THE EMPEROR'S GUEST

is Don Peacock's diary of 1276 days as a British prisoner of war of the Japanese in Indonesia during World War II, spent mainly as a white coolie on the tropical island of Haruku. The tale opens in Singapore as the young Yorkshireman is patriotically drinking gin, to prevent it from falling into enemy hands. Fleeing on a ship bound for Australia, he is ordered off in Batavia (now Jakarta) to defend Java, but the island surrenders and, after rejecting a guerrilla life behind Japanese lines, he is persuaded to join a slave-labour battalion.

After conversion to a rice diet, and toughening up to withstand Nip brutality, he joins a party transforming Haruku into an aircraft carrier. The island of disease, despair and death is run by a half-crazed Nip sergeant as his own little kingdom. Survivors run the gauntlet of American bombers and submarines to regain Java. The author is bound for Indo-China when the Allies blocked the Seas and he ends his war in Singapore.

DONALD PEACOCK was born at Stapleton, N. Yorks., in 1919, and educated at Darlington Grammar School in County Durham. His career as a trainee journalist on the *Northern Despatch* was interrupted when he was called up for World War II a week before Chamberlain even blew the whistle.

After his years as a guest of the Emperor, he returned to journalism, retiring in 1984 as deputy night editor at the *Daily Mirror*'s Manchester office. Don Peacock married in 1948, and has a son and daughter. His first wife died in 1976. He now lives with his second wife in Cheshire.

☆

The Emperor's Guest

The Diary of a British Prisoner-of-War of the
Japanese in Indonesia

Don Peacock

Introduced by Derek Jameson

Oleander

The Oleander Press
17 Stansgate Avenue
Cambridge CB2 2QZ
England

The Oleander Press
210 Fifth Avenue
New York, N.Y. 10010
U.S.A.

British Library Cataloguing in Publication Data

Peacock, Donald Robert
The Emperor's Guest: the diary of a British prisoner-of-war of
the Japanese in Indonesia.
1. Japan. British prisoners of war, 1939-1945 –
Biographies
I. Title
940.54′72′520924

ISBN 0–906672–55–4

Printed and bound in Great Britain

Contents

Acknowledgements

The author wishes to express his grateful thanks for their help in providing illustrations to ex-comrades Dave Harries, Ammanford; Martin Ofield, Chesterfield; Leo Rawlings, Berkhamsted; Ron Thompson, Gatley; and the artist who drew the sketches of Wing-Commander Gregson, 'Nitty Whiskers', and Gunzo Mori, whom it has been impossible to trace.

Thanks are due also to the Associated Press and the artist Montague Black for the 'Bomb over Hiroshima' painting; to the Camera Press of London for the 'Dream of Bali' photograph; to the Sport and General Agency, London, for 'Dobbin Goes to War'; and to the Trustees of the Imperial War Museum, London, for the photographs attributed to them in the list of illustrations.

Introduction

God knows what they are teaching in our schools these days. The history of World War II certainly doesn't appear to loom large in the curriculum. *Lest We Forget* went up the heartfelt cry after the last holocaust and the one before that. Say it today and people will wonder what you are talking about.

Perhaps the saddest thing about the rumpus over that decision to send the Duke of Edinburgh to the funeral of Emperor Hirohito of Japan early in 1989 was that the argument was lost on millions born in the past forty years.

'I thought the war was against the Germans,' said one young lady of my acquaintance. Since the Japanese have so easily conquered us with the television set, video recorder and motor car, I suppose people can be forgiven for overlooking the fact that they swept all before them with more lethal efficiency a few decades earlier.

Having already overrun large areas of China and Indochina, Japan eagerly joined Hitler's war on 7 December, 1941, with the surprise attack on America's Pacific headquarters at Pearl Harbour. Within a year the Japanese had crushed the British, American and Dutch forces who ruled over much of Southeast Asia.

The Rising Sun of the Nipponese empire flew from the borders of India to the very doorstep of Australia in the name of the aforementioned Hirohito, 124th direct descendant of Japan's first ruler and the greatest warlord of them all. Only in recent times did he change from sun of heaven to quiet, scholarly marine biologist. The Americans who finally atom-bombed the Japs into submission decided that image would be healthier for the nation's post-war recovery.

Don Peacock's timely story puts history into perspective. He was never left in any doubt about the imperial sanctity of Hirohito as, near starvation and stricken with malaria and dysentery, he managed somehow to stay alive as an RAF erk who fell prisoner to Japan's conquering armies. Or, as one of his captors put it more grandiosely, 'a guest of the Emperor.'

This guest was the kind that bad hosts like least. He happened to be a journalist well qualified to tell his story, made all the more damning by the fact that it was written furtively in shorthand on scraps of paper. If discovered, they could literally have cost the author his head.

The Japs certainly had plenty to hide. Don Peacock presents yet more evidence of their barbaric savagery in the treatment of prisoners. It suited their wartime purpose to worship the notion that men of honour and dignity stood and died where they fought. Those who failed the ultimate test by staying alive and falling prisoner rated no higher than dirt under a fingernail.

Our men were treated accordingly. Of 50,016 British servicemen captured, no fewer than 12,433 died in Japanese hands of malnutrition, disease and, in many cases, cold-blooded murder. A large number of those who did get back home never recovered normal health. It was the same story with American, Australian, Dutch and prisoners of another dozen nationalities fighting the Allied cause.

Don Peacock suffered it all. For $3\frac{1}{2}$ years he toiled long and hard as a coolie labourer. All round him men dropped like flies. He fought death from starvation by foraging for roots and eating slugs. There were many other horrors to endure: watching helplessly as friends succumbed; the threat of summary execution for daring to step out of line; the thwack of rifle butt on a broken body.

For all that, Don tells his terrible tale with much humour and little bitterness. Never once does he complain about his lot, though he admits ruefully in passing that he could have stayed in Blighty instead of becoming store-basher in a RAF motor repair section in doomed Singapore.

I know Don Peacock well. He worked alongside me in the 'Seventies as a production executive when I was Northern editor of the *Daily Mirror* in Manchester. He is one of the best. A quiet, reflective man who gets on with it and is not given to swinging the lamp. I didn't even know Don had been a Pow until this remarkable manuscript came into my hands.

His is a story of the human spirit triumphing against the most fearful odds. Should there be any Japanese out there who believe that honour and dignity lie only in a warrior's death, let them read the story of Leading Aircraftman Peacock, D.R., 747461. They will learn much.

Derek Jameson.

DEREK JAMESON

Foreword

In the RAF the lowest forms of life are, or at any rate were in my day, the erks. Erks don't generally write war books. That's the prerogative of the heroes and the top brass, which under normal circumstances is all very right and proper. Heroes have their stirring tales to tell; the top brass, hopefully, have some idea of what we were all supposed to be doing. But in the bizarre, often quite incredible, world of the Far East prison camps, live heroes were far and few between: the Nips saw to that. And the top brass were, to all intents and purposes, reduced to the ranks. So, in these special circumstances I offer an erk's diary.

I kept up my diary throughout my three and a half years as a guest of the Emperor, as one of the less obnoxious of our hosts once described it. In parts, particularly those entries made during the early days, it is quite detailed. Later its contents deteriorated with the conditions in the camps. I soon filled my original notebook, so something to write on became a constant problem. As paper was nigh on non-existent, I had to compete for odd scraps, stolen from the Nips, with nicotine addicts who wanted them to roll cigarettes from the local weed.

I also felt more than slightly inhibited in what I wrote in case the Nips took an interest in it. I didn't think they would ever read my shorthand, as I have great difficulty in reading it myself, but I certainly had no desire to risk having my head chopped off, even in the interests of posterity.

I wrote of what seemed important to me at the time. For instance I assiduously recorded the wild rumours which we eagerly swallowed. They may seem absurd now, but they were important then because they kept our hopes alive. I hope my diary does not dwell too much on the lighter moments in the grim battle for survival. I am acutely aware that only 750 of the 2075 men who went to Haruku came home. But life wasn't all unrelieved misery, and I'm sure that an ability to see the humour of our situation helped many to survive.

I first roughed my book out some forty years ago. I'd got the material, and I thought I might have the ability, but fell short on dedication. I typed out large chunks but kept getting distracted by such mundane matters as labouring for the monthly pay cheque, washing nappies or painting the house. Progress wasn't helped by the fact that I'm an incredibly slow worker and bad typist. The years rolled on, and at my retirement the project still stayed on the drawing board. Then, robbed of the excuse that I had no time to write, I felt I simply had to complete it if just to prove that I could really do it.

Just one more point. As a prisoner I always referred to our captors as the Nips, and I see no reason to change now. This is in no way intended to be derogatory. To them their country was Nippon, not Japan, and I reckon they would as soon be Nips as Japs.

D.R. PEACOCK

Illustrations

Prisoners wait anxiously for their rice at a five-star officers-only prison camp. But no doubt the battle for 'leggi' was just as intense, if a little more restrained, as on Haruku. (Imperial War Museum)   101

The envelope that brought a tear to the author's eye. Amazingly this despairing address was enough to find him some eighteen months later half a world away in Haruku. And it didn't even have a stamp on it   112

So peaceful now in this Dave Harries picture, but on December 7, 1943, a squadron of bombers came plummeting out of the clouds above this jetty and blasted the village in the background. Prisoners spent December 8 searching the smouldering ruins for bodies   115

Diary extract from February 12, 1944, ten months after arriving on Haruku   121

The Gunzo's nightmare. If Mori was the little king of Haruku, he was a moody, sullen king. Perhaps he foresaw the day when, as in this photo, he himself would be the prisoner. Here he is on the right, without his bamboo pole, without his dark glasses but with Kasi Yama still beside him, after surrendering in Java   122

Part of the diary which Don Peacock kept during the whole of his imprisonment. During searches he put it in a prominent position to make sure it was ignored. The edges of the bag he kept it in are tattered where he unthreaded the canvas for sewing cotton   135

Once the scene here was reminiscent of the building of the Pyramids with hundreds of Pow slaves toiling under the Nip lash to provide an advance base for Hirohito's warplanes. But Dave Harries found that although Haruku now has electricity and a road the bush has reclaimed the airfield   137

The Lockheed Lightning P38 (San-ju-achi to the Nips) which escorted the bombers raiding Ambon. It was also responsible for Don Peacock's sprained ankle, sustained when he leapt into a latrine to avoid its cannon fire. (Imperial War Museum)   143

Artist-author Leo Rawlings who worked on the Burma railway, entitled this picture "Will It Never End?" (1949) which admirably sums up the feelings of the Haruku survivors when told they were being shipped out to work in Indo-China   159

'Banana money' as the Singapore Chinese called it, which rolled off the Nip presses in the occupied territories without even serial numbers. Its value gradually became less and less until it was declared worthless at the end of the war   169

The Emperor's Guest

1: FLIGHT FROM DESTINY

February - March, 1942.   Singapore and Java

One of my clearer recollections of school is of the oak panels
around the assembly hall with their hundreds of names, in gilt
lettering, of old boys who had died in WWI. Perusing those lists
during the tedious ritual of morning prayers, to my surprise I
stumbled across another D.R. Peacock. The discovery sprang viv-
idly to mind a few years later when there seemed more than a faint
chance of my qualifying to join my namesake on the wall. Such
dull repetition, I decided, should be avoided at all costs.

It was a warm and sunny afternoon in Singapore, but as I stared
out across the coconut palms and banana trees to the brilliant blue
sea I felt a chill. Out of the cloudless sky a Nip dive bomber came
plummeting down, totally unchallenged, towards the grey hulk of
a large troopship, already gushing out ominous black smoke. As
the ship vanished in a cloud of spray I turned in my wicker chair
for another gulp of gin, but the chipped enamel mug was empty.
Well, I didn't really like the stuff anyway. Trouble was there were
crates of it outside the planter's bungalow we were using as a
billet. And in 1942 everyone had to do his bit. It would never do to
let the Nips get hold of all that booze! The gin was one of the few
things that Britain had managed to salvage out of the disaster of
Malaya. Some truck-driver or other had hung on to it as he fled
down the peninsula just in front of the advancing enemy. Here in
Singapore he had run out of road, and his truck and the gin were
now in the care of the RAF's No 1 Transport Repair Section, high
up on Bukit Timah, the island's nearest approach to a mountain.

1

Don Peacock on the verandah of his billet at RAF Seletar, Singapore. It was bomb
shrapnel raking this verandah that awakened him in the early hours of December 7,
1941 to the fact that Nips had opened hostilities

No 1 MTRS was hardly a fighting unit, and I was wondering what the hell we were doing here. The RAF, whose vehicles we were supposed to be servicing, appeared to have been long since shot out of the skies. Intermittent shells screamed overhead, and the Nips were only a mile of two away over the top of our hill. It was all like a scene from one of the blood and thunder films I'd been watching back home not so very long before, except that here the good guys always seemed to come off worse.

A few weeks earlier, at RAF Seletar, I'd watched the *Prince of Wales* and *Repulse* sail off down the Straits of Johore to show the Nips just who ruled the waves. Within 48 hours enemy torpedo bombers had sent them to the bottom of the South China Sea. I'd seen Seletar's open-cockpit Vickers Wildebeests fly out to cool the Nips' ardour with a few well-directed high explosives. I never saw the planes again.

Then, here at Bukit Timah, I'd heard the blast as the causeway linking Singapore to the mainland was cut to leave an impassable moat in the path of the Nips. It scarcely caused them to pause for breath.

Fortunately I was not the only one a trifle concerned about the future of our little unit. There were no flies on our tubby Aussie CO. He found some pretext to phone Air Headquarters, down in the comparative safety of the city. "Oh, sorry," they said. "We'd forgotten about you. Still at Bukit Timah are you? Better get out ... fast."

But first secret documents had to be destroyed. It would never have done for the two Nip divisions who stormed our hill two nights later to have learned that Truck S13 was due for a service, or that S25 had just had its brakes relined. I spent an anxious afternoon stoking the fire. Then we, and as many vehicles as we could move, joined the milling thousands on the Bukit Timah road who were trying to get to, or away from, the front line. Almost the whole of the British forces in the Far East seemed to be bumbling about in the blackout there that night. Somehow we managed to get our vehicles down to Tanjong Pagar docks just as dawn was breaking. And what a fantastic dawn! The rising sun floodlit a huge smoke plume spiralling over the abandoned Naval Base, transforming this man-made cloud into gigantic marble bubbles of blue, purple, red, orange and yellow.

Our orders were to get our transport aboard ship and report to AHQ for further instructions. There was only one vessel in sight:

a long, grey, forbidding-looking cargo liner with the lettering *Empire Star, Belfast* on her stern. I don't think I'm particularly superstitious but I read ships' names like fortune-tellers read palms. Some conjure up sunny Caribbean cruises, others exhilarating record-breaking voyages across the North Atlantic. But *Empire Star* smacked of bloody tales of Chinese pirates or hopeless battles against typhoons. And, as if to confirm my forebodings, the sirens wailed for what had become Singapore's routine pre-breakfast air raid. Which brings me to another superstition: one I readily admit to. I believe it extremely unlucky to be caught in the vicinity of docks during an air raid. But this time there was no more than a smattering of bombs. And after the drone of aircraft had died away the day sprang to life.

The *Empire Star's* derricks began swinging cargo aboard, but she seemed in no hurry for our trucks. We cooked a meal of sorts on the dockside, dodged the odd bomb and hung about, wearily. A few soldiers scavenged in the wrecked, burning godowns. They came out waving electric clocks and, what seemed more interesting, beer and cigarettes. A fleeing rubber-planter dangled his car keys in front of us, offering his shiny new Chevrolet to anyone who cared to take it. No one did. What little British-held road there was to run on was diminishing hourly.

Nothing was of much value now except squatting room on a ship. Any ship... even the *Empire Star*. Another night dossing down on the docks. Then an interminable day. The island was in its final agonies now. Bombs, shells, and, everywhere, fires. Mains were fractured and there was no water for the fire hoses. We finally got our transport aboard ship. A despatch-rider was sent to AHQ for further orders. He was soon back, having found the building ablaze and abandoned.

Our CO needed no further bidding. He had discovered by this time that the *Empire Star* was bound first for Batavia (now Jakarta) and then his home town, Sydney. He ordered us aboard. We scrambled eagerly up on deck, hunting for somewhere to sit among the crowd of civilian men, women and children, nurses, British and Australian troops and a few Marines. In a stupor of incredulity at all that had happened during the past few weeks, we waited, impatient to get away. But the *Empire Star*, which appeared to be the only ship in the docks, stayed put. It was not until dusk the following day that she began to move away. All that time more refugees had been piling aboard. And still they came, right up to the last second, abandoning their pitiful bundles to catch and shin up the trailing mooring ropes as we left the quayside.

On a rocky islet not far out to sea we saw our first British plane for several days, a crashed fighter, its wings washed by the waves. It was one of the Hurricanes which had come too late and too few in numbers to stem the Nip advance. To our dismay, instead of putting as many nautical miles as possible between us and Singapore under cover of darkness, the *Empire Star* dropped anchor only a mile or two off shore. And it was dawn before we finally saw the island disappear over the horizon. The invading Nip general, Yamashita, had already called for its surrender. It came three days later. As we headed south we were joined by four more ships and a naval escort. It was about 8 a.m. when the first planes appeared. They came at us almost immediately, dive-bombing and machine-gunning. As the largest ship in the convoy the *Empire Star* seemed to come in for special attention.

A direct hit with an HE, just forward of where I was sheltering, sent me sprawling. By the time I had crawled round to recover my specs there was a fire from an incendiary burning on the deck just outside the nearest porthole. I couldn't make up my mind whether to get out on deck ready to leap overboard if we sank, or to stay put, with some protection from shrapnel and machine-gun bullets, and hope for the best. Fortunately not everyone was as useless as I and, while I was dithering, the fire was brought under control. Then another HE hit us amidship. The world seemed to stop. There was utter silence. The ship seemed dead. Then, to my overwhelming relief, the throb of the engines, the very heartbeat of the ship, reasserted itself. The *Empire Star* and nearly all of us aboard remained alive. The more mathematically-minded estimated the number of planes that had hit us at eighty to a hundred. I was too busy trying to keep out of harm's way to count. One, I was told, was shot down, but I missed that too. I don't think it was hit by the AA gun on our ship because one of the blokes supposed to be firing it was lying beside me, keeping his head well down. After what seemed a lifetime, which I spent mostly contemplating how much more comfortable it was to be bombed on dry land, which was unlikely to sink and, in any case, generally offered the bomber a reasonably wide choice of targets to aim at, the dive

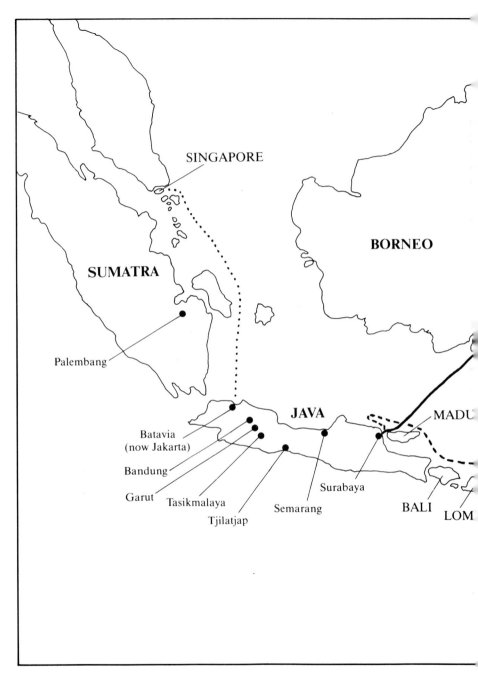

Map of South-East Asia

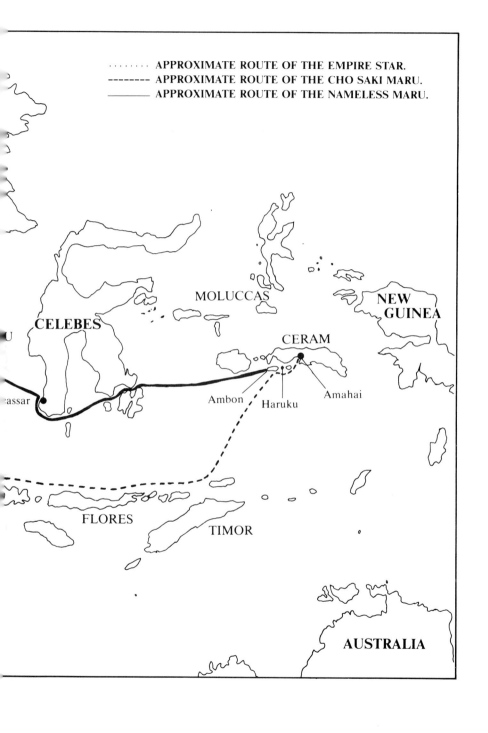

APPROXIMATE ROUTE OF THE EMPIRE STAR.
APPROXIMATE ROUTE OF THE CHO SAKI MARU.
APPROXIMATE ROUTE OF THE NAMELESS MARU.

MOLUCCAS

NEW GUINEA

CELEBES

CERAM

Ambon   Haruku   Amahai

assar

FLORES

TIMOR

AUSTRALIA

bombing ceased.

The Nips now concentrated on high-level attacks. Fortunately the *Empire Star* had a skipper with a keen eye and an iron nerve. He watched for the sticks of bombs leaving the planes, then swung his ship round to a new tack clear of their path. Sometimes we only just made it, and bombs exploding uncomfortably close sent shrapnel scything through the ship's sides. An Aussie lying next but one to me was carried out leaving a pool of blood behind. But, for the most part, the skipper was bang on with his calculations and suffered no more direct hits. Then, about one, the Nips knocked off for lunch.

It was not the happiest of afternoons. Our little group spent a very uneasy hour down in the bowels of the ship somewhat belatedly draining the petrol out of our trucks. And for the rest of the time we sat on deck straining our eyes for the sight we least wanted to see. But dusk came with still no sign of a new attack. The dead, thanks to astonishing good luck and a remarkable skipper, numbering only fourteen, were lowered quietly over the side. There was a short service. We sang *Abide with Me* with lumps in our throats, and thanked God we could still do so. Just to temper any undue optimism some humorist pointed out the date. It was Thursday the 12th, with Friday the 13th coming up and another 24 hours' sailing needed to get us to port.

The next day was my longest Friday ever. From the moment the brilliant tropical sunrise floodlit our fugitive ship, and on throughout the morning when her great foaming, sparkling white wake drew a huge arrow across that bluest of seas, pointing us out to even the blindest of bombers, the day crawled painfully from minute to minute. But as the minutes grew into hours, and noon passed without the dreaded drone of aircraft, hopes began to rise that the bombers were busy attacking someone else.

It was years later that I heard who that someone was. That Friday the 13th wreaked its havoc on Palembang, not far to the north-west of us in Dutch Sumatra. The Nips blitzed an airfield there, destroying many much-needed planes on the ground, and paving the way for their paratroops to land next day. Another huge chunk of territory was about to fall into their hungry grasp.

Nip planes and naval units took a terrible toll of Allied shipping at this time, but we sailed on unchallenged, and at dusk nosed into Batavia's Tanjong Priok docks, a prayer of thanksgiving in our hearts. There was a mad scramble to get ashore in Java but No 1 MTRS stayed put. We felt none too enthusiastic about putting to sea again and running the gauntlet of the Nip air force and perhaps their navy too, but Bondi beach or somewhere was calling our CO. And we would follow him anywhere provided it was away from the Nips.

For two days we stayed aboard the *Empire Star* at the dockside. Sadly we listened on our radio to reports of the surrender of Singapore. The comrades we had left behind were now prisoners. It was time for a long cruise if we were not to end up in the same bag. But just as the ship was about to cast off, a sudden flurry of activity occurred on the quayside. Some very officious-looking RAF types came hurrying up the gangplank. We had re-established contact with AHQ. No, they said. We certainly couldn't stay aboard. Their orders were that no-one was to leave Java. We must get ashore immediately. So the *Empire Star* sailed on without us... and eventually reached Sydney unscathed.

It was never very clear what we were supposed to do in Batavia, but we took over a garage with a beautiful Eurasian secretary, and an old house with an Indonesian-type shower. The secretary kept a stock of Coca-Cola in her office. We all became addicts, but she had sense to match her looks, and the association was strictly business only. I hadn't much luck with the shower either. It comprised a mossy stone slab to stand on, and a stone trough from which you scooped water to pour over yourself. I slipped on the mossy slab and cut open an eyebrow on the trough: my first war wound. The local hospital put in a couple of stitches and crowned me with an imposing bandage. A bandage that earned me murmurs of sympathy wherever I went, except in the secretary's office.

Apart from the little matter of the blackout, air raids and imminent invasion, Batavia, or at any rate our part of it, was a great place to be in. Scarlet Madagascar flame trees and bright yellow mimosa fringed the wide roads. Frangipani and bougainvillea screened the Europeans' cool and spacious bungalows. In the noisy cafés and swinging cabarets a great welcome awaited Englanders, particularly those sporting bandages. Only the poverty-stricken Dutch troops seemed to have reservations about our presence. They found they could no longer compete for the services of the little donkey-carts with tinkling bells and twinkling oil lamps, to say nothing of the city's other attractions.

For a few brief days we seemed to be in paradise. But this idiots' fiesta came to an abrupt end on March 1. The Nips, we were told, had launched a three-pronged invasion of the island, and were advancing rapidly on the city. General Wavell, briefly our Supreme Commander, had folded his tent and decamped to India. Someone in London, New Delhi, or somewhere equally safe, had kindly offered our services to the Dutch as infantry, or anything else for which they might feel our talents fitted us. The Dutch, rather wisely we thought, said they had no use for us or indeed for the majority of the British servicemen, mostly RAF types without planes or equipment, who had been insanely poured into doomed Java. It was time to start running again.

Fortunately we still had the transport we had brought from Singapore. We loaded our trucks and that evening began what developed into a frenetic eight-day road race up and down the tortuous mountain roads of West Java. About midnight, high up in the cool of the Puntjak pass, we felt we had put sufficient miles between us and the Nips to stop and call for a pint in a swish roadhouse there. Behind the blacked-out windows it was party time in the large bar. The end of the world seemed imminent but the crowd of assorted troops there were determined to have at least one more night out.

The hubbub ceased for a BBC World Service news bulletin. This threw little light on the facts of the war situation but concentrated on a stirring declaration by the ABCD powers (America, Britain, China and the Dutch) that the cowardly attacks of the treacherous Nips would not go unpunished, etc. etc. Then came the four national anthems. We all stood solemnly to attention for the lot. For a few minutes No 1 MTRS had become part of the glorious struggle against the wicked aggressor. Then it was back to our trucks, to start running again.

Around dawn we passed through the beautifully situated ultra modern-city of Bandung. We didn't dally to admire it. Then at lunchtime, in the hot and dusty streets of Tasikmalaya, our freedom dash came to an abrupt halt. Suddenly no-one seemed to know where we were going, or when. We spent the rest of that day and all that night in our trucks at the roadside waiting for orders. It was here that we first heard the Java drums. They began far off in distant hills. Then the insistent throbbing came nearer

Dobbin goes to war. As Java braced itself for invasion the Press was issued with this picture of the Dutch East Indies forces preparing to meet the might of the Nip army and airforce

and nearer, until someone beat out the message on his hollowed-out tree trunk almost in our eardrums. There was not even the hope of a snooze until the drumbeats echoed away through the palm trees and up into the mountains.

Someone suggested that it must be a jungle *News of the World* reporting Java's latest sex scandal. But we knew all too well that the drums heralded the Nip advance, which accounted for the grins on the faces of the natives walking past our trucks.

Our flagging spirits were not improved much when next day the order was handed down from whatever oracle was now guiding our convoy that we were to make a smart about-turn and head back the way we had come.

The next stop on our island tour gave us a second chance to admire the garden city of Bandung, but we weren't much in the mood for sightseeing as we dossed down in our trucks in a main street. We awoke next morning in a ghost city. All the inhabitants seemed to have fled or gone into hiding. But the place was not to be deserted entirely. We had to stay, we were told, and we moved into a school. That evening half a dozen of us, wandering aimlessly in the empty streets, were amazed to find a cinema apparently open for business. Presumably the boss had left in too much of a hurry to tell his staff that all their potential customers had vanished. It felt rather eerie, but we went in. Cinemas take some beating for a quiet nap when you're a dosser. With the whole barn of a place to ourselves we watched, or slept through, a film called quite incredibly *Flight from Destiny*. It seemed like a bad joke.

When we returned to the school all was confusion. The orders from on high were that we were to move out immediately. Our own flight from destiny resumed. We headed east and soon made good progress, not surprisingly considering it was our third trip over this particular piece of Java within 48 hours. We even had some hazy idea of where we hoped to go. The island's main ports, all on her north coast were, according to our CO, now held or blockaded by the Nips. We headed for Tjilatjap, a small port on the south coast where our dream boat was waiting. By this time the Javanese had begun to enjoy the fun. At each kampong crowds began waving and cheering (or was it jeering?) as soon as we drove in sight. Throughout the next night their drums chattered away all around us.

Next day we neared the coast with ever-rising hopes. But within about 20 miles of Tjilatjap our route was blocked by Dutch troops. We were too late. The port had been blitzed, they told us. The Nips had landed and were fanning out in the paddy-fields all around us. We had been running away from the Nips who landed in the west of the island. Now we faced another Nip force who had rather unsportingly landed in the east. It was time for another smart about-turn. Back in the hills, at a place called Tjamis, we stopped. We'd no idea where we were going anyway. We sat on the roadside refreshing ourselves with the juice of young coconuts and discussed what the hell to do next. Of course we could have just set up as a guerrilla band, playing havoc with Nip lines of communication, blowing up ammo dumps, feeding back vital secrets to the Allies, perhaps changing the whole course of the war in the Pacific.

In fact that is more or less what Churchill seemed to have had in mind for us. In a farewell cable he sent us his "best wishes for success and honour in the great fight that confronts you." But there were snags.

We hadn't even the rudimentary knowledge of the country around us.

We couldn't speak the language.

We didn't know where the Nips were, let alone their lines of communication.

And, in any case, no-one had bothered to pass on Churchill's message.

Against all that, it was a beautiful day for a guerrilla campaign, and the scenery was simply magnificent. But we hadn't entirely given up hope. We still had the crazy idea that if we could find a quiet stretch of coastline we might yet be picked up by an Allied ship. Or, failing that, perhaps we could sail, step by step, along that chain of islands that links Java with Australia... or more or less anyway.

We just didn't realise that the war had swept on past us. That the Allies had been driven from all neighbouring seas by their rout in the Battle of the Java Sea. That the Nips had seized Bali, our first stepping-stone to Australia, landed on Timor, the last one, and had already bombed Australia itself. We were now many hundreds of miles behind the lines.

We armed ourselves by buying a parang apiece from the natives at, of course, several times its market value, and drove hopefully on. It was now Sunday, March 8. Approaching a place we had identified as Garut on our map, we spotted a large convoy coming through the hills in the opposite direction. After reassuring ourselves that it was one of ours, we pulled into the side of the road to wait for it. It turned out to be the remnants of the RAF's Far East Command, who presumably were also unaware of Churchill's message. They had orders for us, not from Churchill, but from the

Nips. All British forces were to throw down their arms, if any. Otherwise they would be shot on sight. Our group was to proceed to Tasikmalaya airfield.

The Dutch had surrendered the East Indies.

We slung our newly-acquired parangs into a river and joined the convoy to captivity. In every kampong along the road happy crowds watched us pass. The Nips' flag was sprouting everywhere. Like ourselves, the Javanese had a lot to learn about the new masters of Asia. So far, among our little group, no-one had suffered much more than wounded pride. But we had been lucky, thanks mainly to having had our own transport available when the dash for Tjilatjap began. Less fortunate RAF groups made for Tjilatjap by train. Like us they arrived too late. Like us they made a smart about-turn. But from there on their war became real and bloody.

It was then dark, and they hadn't got very far before the train was ambushed by Nip infantry, who raked the coaches with bullets. Many men were hit, but the engine, though leaking water, kept going long enough to carry the rest out of immediate danger. It finally spluttered to a halt. The more seriously injured were taken to some nearby huts which were quickly turned into a makeshift Red Cross hospital. The rest of the party began marching along the rail track away from the Nips.

Not far along the railway, unaware of the fate of the train, Dutch troops stood guard at a bridge, awaiting the Nips, with dynamite charges in position. In the darkness they mistook the approaching British for the enemy. When the group got on to the bridge the Dutch blew it up. About the same time the Nips found the Red Cross huts and massacred their occupants.

2: THE BRYLCREEM MARTYRS

March - May, 1942.   Tasikmalaya, Java

For anyone who had to be a prisoner-of-war Tasikmalaya was as good a place as any to start. The spine of Java is more like a setting for an Oriental *Sound of Music* than a *Colditz*-type drama. It's a lush green land of volcanoes, some thickly wooded, others with terraced ricefields climbing like giant stairways way up towards their summits.

Tasik airfield lay in a bowl in the hills, surrounded by orderly paddy-fields, palm groves and flame-of-the-forest trees. For those who cared to look there were exotic birds, shiny lizards and fantastic butterflies. Each evening flying foxes, giant fruit bats, would slowly wing across the sky, silhouetted against the dying sunset, en route to their feeding grounds.

But before deciding whether to pass our days of captivity bird-watching or collecting butterflies, we had more mundane matters to attend to, like finding somewhere to sleep and something to eat. Neither presented much difficulty.

We installed ourselves in a couple of large empty hangars. There was water on tap. Most of us had a very essential mosquito net, a blanket and some clothing. We found sufficient junk lying around for us to knock up some sort of beds. So in no time at all each of us was busy transforming his own personal few square feet of concrete into home.

As for grub, well we might not have exactly distinguished ourselves on the field of battle, but we did know that an army marches (or maybe nowadays it should be rides) on its stomach. At Tasik, nearly everyone, about 2000 of us, had arrived by road. And each group had loaded its trucks with whatever rations it had been able to lay its hand on. True it was mostly bully-beef and tinned potatoes, but that's not a bad foundation on which to build a meal. Also, while the Javanese might have been tumbling over themselves to show their love of the Nips and hatred of the Allies, they weren't going to let their new loyalties prevent their making a fast buck. Almost before our trucks had stopped rolling the kampong entrepreneurs were setting up shop at the camp fence. There were blue eggs, sun-dried fish and a wide variety of tropical fruits and veg for sale, all at utterly exorbitant prices. We paid up and started off prison camp life in grand style.

In fact we could have lived happily ever after but for one slight problem: the Nips. They first disturbed our peace on our second day on the airfield. We were lined up on one of those wretched parades without which, unfortunately, Service life seems quite unable to function, when a formation of bombers, with fighters weaving behind them, came screaming in at us little more than palm high.

Every nerve in our bodies urged us to dive for cover as we had learned to do over the past three months. The ranks wavered, but the officer in charge, moustache bristling, his face puce with anger, bawled at us to stand fast. And when it came to the choice of facing the bombers or the wrath of the wing-commander, it had to be the bombers. We stood there petrified as the planes kept diving at us. Quite likely, we reasoned, their pilots had been bombing and strafing as long as we had been ducking and running. Could they now kick that unfortunate habit? They could and they did. A few more low passes over the parade, and off they flew.

A few days later we met our hosts eyeball to eyeball. It was late afternoon. The camp was just stirring into activity after a long siesta when a totally unexpected lorry bedecked with Nip flags and loaded with armed troops came racing across the airfield. It pulled up among a group of us. We stared at the Nips. The Nips stared at us. They crouched along the sides of the truck, scruffy and undersized, holding their rifles grimly between their knees. In their washed-out uniforms, with cloth streamers dangling from their peaked hats like tatty pigtails, they could scarcely have looked less like conquering heroes.

Gradually a curious crowd gathered around them. The silent battle of stares intensified. Then, neither side meeting quite the hostility it feared, eased off again. The swarthy faces began to relax. Here and there came the suspicion of a smile. Despite our inner feelings some of us grinned back. This was apparently what the Nips wanted. Simply beaming now, they quickly moved into the rôle of indulgent victors. Soon they were all jabbering away at once. So many of them spoke intelligible English that it seemed obvious that they had been specially picked for this reconnaissance, for that was what it amounted to. For the moment they all seemed anxious to please: over-anxious perhaps. Some even went so far as to throw us cigarettes, which weren't refused. For a few more minutes they simply oozed goodwill. Then they drove off as suddenly as they had arrived. Presumably they went back to report that we were a pretty docile bunch unlikely to cause much trouble. They had performed their rôle efficently. No doubt they would have done their duty just as adequately had they been sent in to mow us down.

Their softly, softly approach came as a big surprise, but looking back nothing could have been more rational. A huge empire had fallen into the Nips' grasp within a matter of weeks. They had the whole of the East Indies from Sumatra to New Guinea to bring under control, not to mention the Philippines and sundry island groups all over the South Pacific, and seemed quite happy to leave the matter of a couple of thousand disarmed and demoralised Brits in the pending tray. But we were not entirely forgotten. A few days later Nip guards set up shop at the camp gates. They checked how many fish they had in this particular net, and casually mentioned that for every man who escaped six others would be shot. Then, for the time being, we were left to our own devices.

We became a trifle uneasy about the shootings threat when we found that an enterprising group of aircrew types were busy trying to repair a damaged American bomber that had been left in a corner of the airfield. The affair put our senior officers on the spot. Should they help the aircrew to carry out their undoubted duty to try to escape; or act to protect those who would be left to face the music, if not the firing squad?

Here we had reached the point where in your Hollywood war epic those to be left behind nobly rise as one man and insist that the would-be escapees should get their chance, and indeed offer them every assistance.

With us, I'm afraid, it wasn't quite like that. There were mutterings that this wildcat scheme should not be allowed to put our necks at risk. Wasn't the future grim enough without deliberately inviting trouble? The issue was finally settled when the officers sent a party of only-too-willing volunteers to slash the bomber's tyres and sabotage any hope of getting it off the ground.

The frustrated flyers were not too happy about this. They swore to see that those responsible were court-martialled as soon as we were freed. But freedom proved much farther away than any of us dreamed, even in our most despairing moments. With no escape bid and no shootings we continued to make the best of this period of phoney captivity. We set about organising the sort of activities we thought Pows were supposed to indulge in.

Gardens to keep us in veg seemed a good idea. We started digging in the fond hope that Tasikmalaya was to be our permanent home. Then we felt no good prison camp would be complete without its home-produced entertainments, so we got up a concert. A secret radio was a must. Our officers produced one. I went along each day to take down as much of the BBC Overseas Service news as my inadequate shorthand would allow. The result was the *Tasikmalaya Times*, which an officer read out to anyone interested. The news was always terrible, though everyone was interested to hear that London had us still up in the hills harassing the enemy in the true Churchillian spirit. Of course there had to be some sporting activities. Some officers took up hunting: hunting the flies which bred in fantastic numbers in the open trench latrines we had dug. Enthusiasts set themselves a target of 500 a day. The champ, I think a fighter pilot, set up a record kill of 94 at one swipe, using slightly-off bullybeef as bait.

Then there were shopping expeditions to the fence. So far the Nips had shown no interest in our private market. I made one important purchase. I bought one of those large plate-shaped basket-work hats worn by natives in the paddyfields. It brought a few ribald comments, and hints that the sun had got me already, but had I been able to foretell the future I could not have made a better buy.

Most of our companions had come into prison camp more or less straight off the boat from Liverpool, pausing only for a quick pint in a Batavia bar. So we old hands wiled away pleasant hours hunting out newcomers from our hometowns who could tell us if the Odeon was still standing and if they still had the same barmaid in the Red Lion.

There was more than a little consternation when our rations ran out and the Nips began supplying rice instead of spuds. This may seem a minor problem to present-day generations weaned on Chinese takeaways, but for many of us it was disaster. It wouldn't have been so bad if our cooks had possessed some idea of how to make the stuff palatable, but they hadn't. It came up either like warm gravel or thick glue. We cushioned the switch to a rice-based diet by forming cook groups. Group members pooled cash to buy supplies at the fence, lit their own fire and cooked weird but not unsatisfying meals in utensils made out of tins from the last of the British rations. At last there was a real test for the RAF mess-tin I had been carrying around for the past three years. I tried a fry-up in it, and ended up with an omelette of molten lead. Obviously it had been manufactured more with kit inspections in mind than cooking.

Slowly the Nips began to make their presence felt. They quizzed aircrew on how British fighters could find enemy bombers in the dark. And they didn't take kindly to the suggestion that it was all done with carrots. Although we were all too well aware of the Nips' reputation, it sent a shock wave round the camp when a wing-commander was taken away for questioning and failed to return.

The Nips also began calling for working parties. Nothing drastic, just a few men to fill in bomb craters and repair roads. But it was the first sign of what was to be our new rôle in life. Soon they were demanding drivers to collect the various stores which had been left strewn around the airfield. This was easier than pick and shovel work, so after a while, although my only two previous attempts at motoring had ended in disaster, I promoted myself to driver. The first passengers I carried ignobly abandoned my pick-up truck and walked, but, as I told them, everyone has to learn.

The airfield was littered with abandoned vehicles of all descriptions. The Nips decided they would like them all taken to Bandung, and asked for more drivers. To a true patriot this might smack of collaboration with the enemy, but for many it seemed stupid to miss a chance to get away from camp and see what was happening in the great Nip world outside. I modestly decided that the 40-odd-mile drive was a bit beyond my capabilities, but there was no shortage of volunteers. They returned from the first trip jubilant. Bandung's Dutch women had not been interned and if the city's streets had not actually flowed with milk and honey, they'd certainly been swimming with beer, to say nothing of cigarettes and cakes. There was a bottle of beer for me, too, brought back by my friend Jim. But, tragically, after bringing it all the way from Bandung, he let it slip out of his hands as I greeted him, and it smashed on the floor at my feet. Men came from all over the camp that night to visit my bit of concrete and savour once again that pub-type stale beer aroma. For me the only solution seemed to be to go for my own booze. Jim flatteringly reckoned that I could make the trip. So when the next convoy left I was with it, at the wheel of a small pick-up truck, with which I was now reasonably familiar. There were just a couple of problems. I'd never driven up a hill and the truck's self-starter was out of action.

I bowled along fairly comfortably on the flat, but the switch-back mountain roads were just not up to my style of driving. I couldn't get the hang of changing down and every time we hit a sharp incline, which was frequently, I stalled. I had made sure that I got a place in the convoy well out of sight of the Nips, who formed the nose and the tail, but if I had to keep getting out to crank the engine I was going to be in deep trouble. Jim partially solved the problem by sticking on my tail and punting my truck in the rear to restart it each time I stopped. This proved very time-consuming. I slipped farther and farther back in the convoy, and nearer and nearer the following Nips. Jim pointed out the only solution. What ground I lost uphill I must regain downhill. So it was foot down and hope for the best as we raced round one hairpin bend after another.

Fortunately the new Nip regime seemed to have cleared all civilian motor traffic off the roads, so the chance of meeting oncoming traffic was small. But round one corner I roared quite unexpectedly into a kampong in the throes of market day. There were bullock carts, hens, goats and their owners all over the road. Somehow I shot safely though the lot, leaving only angry shouts and clenched fists to mark my passage.

I nearly made it to Bandung, but not quite. Somewhere near the end of the journey my truck decided to skid off the road and end up bogged down in a swamp. It was a piece of such incredibly bad driving that I was left scared to death that I was going to die a hero... shot for sabotage.

I waited, in a decidedly unheroic state of mind, for the Nips to arrive, the faithful Jim standing by. But our guards were in a hurry. They didn't seem to care that I might be a dangerous saboteur. They just didn't want to be delayed. Perhaps they had so many captured vehicles to cope with that they were delighted that I had been good enough to relieve them of one. Anyway they ordered me to hop up alongside Jim, and I rode thankfully into Bandung as his passenger.

Then came the big letdown. There was no beer, no cigarettes, no cakes and indeed no sign whatsoever of the Dutch women who had greeted the previous convoy. We didn't actually see any signs saying "Don't feed the prisoners" but no doubt the Nips had made it very clear that they would not tolerate any repetition of the earlier picnic. We returned emptyhanded to Tasik in a mosquito bus driven by a kamikaze-type Nip determined to run down some luckless peasant's chicken even if it meant driving more off the road than on it in order to do so.

The days crawled on to Easter Sunday, a great occasion for the padre who had been captured with us. So far he had found most of us a reluctant flock, but here, even in a prison camp, arose an unchallengable excuse for a church parade. He had found a text that might have been specially written for us. And as he quoted "I will lift up mine eyes unto the hills from whence cometh my help," many looked almost involuntarily towards the mountains around us with high hopes that they would soon echo to the pipes of a new Havelock racing to the Relief of Tasikmalaya. It was as well that we were unaware that that very day the Allies, so far from worrying about Java, were fighting to defend Ceylon from a Nip fleet bombing and sinking ships there.

However we didn't have to pin our hopes exclusively on Biblical deliverance. Some of the traders at the fence handed out an ancient prophecy with the tapioca roots. A Javanese legend, we were told, said the island would be invaded by a race of little men (who else but the Nips?) but that their rule would last only the time between two rice harvests. A little more research at the fence pinned this down to a hundred days. So we started counting. Few of us dreamt that we could be prisoners any longer than that. We couldn't afford to, because the Nips were now beginning to show a keener interest in us.

We were each given a tin badge with a number on it, and ordered to wear it at all times. The badges made us feel like little orphans on a day's outing, but at least they did give us some sort of assurance that we were now officially recognised as Pows. We had been uneasy about this because the Nips, so far from accepting the Geneva Convention on Pows, had seemed reluctant to admit that any such animals existed. They demanded that their own troops should die rather than surrender, and no doubt felt that we should have done likewise, if only to save them embarrassment. However Pow No 2302 was still very much alive and had every intention of staying that way.

Perhaps it was our new status that gave our officers the strange notion that we were entitled to a few of the necessities of life, even if we had to buy them ourselves. They submitted to the Nips a shopping list on which, in a moment of lunacy, someone had included combs.

The following day a terrible rumour spead round the camp. The Nips had ordered us to be shorn like sheep, or at anyrate like Nips. To us RAF types (we weren't called the Brylcreem Boys for nothing) this was the ultimate humiliation. The first martyrs went to the chair next morning. Many a brave man bit his lip as his tresses were strewn on the floor around him. By nightfall next day we were a hangarful of Kojaks.

The RAF were not called the Brylcreem Boys for nothing. Even Don Peacock, not exactly a leader of fashion, had his waves as his Malaya identity card shows. The order to be shorn like sheep, or at any rate like Nips, was for many the ultimate humiliation

The Nips then began tightening the screw. They started with a search of the camp for radios. Our last link with home was tossed hurriedly down a well.

Next, on May 17, large numbers of armed Nips, with bayonets fixed, moved into the hangars, and held us under strict guard. A batch of 500 of us, Jim and I included, was told to be ready to move out next morning, destination unknown. This separated us from the rest of No 1 MTRS, and I've never heard anything of them since.

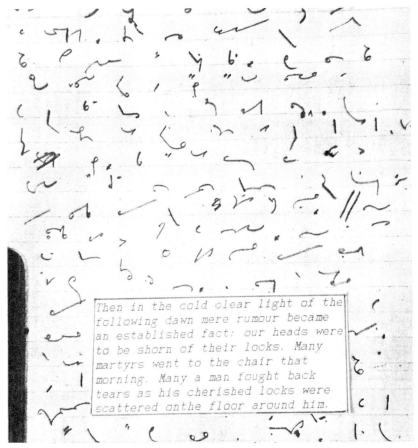

Then in the cold clear light of the following dawn mere rumour became an established fact: our heads were to be shorn of their locks. Many martyrs went to the chair that morning. Many a man fought back tears as his cherished locks were scattered on the floor around him.

Diary extract from the days of phoney imprisonment and blissful ignorance in April, 1942

The Nips made it a 'See the White Coolies' carnival for the locals when they marched the author through Tasikmalaya. Here they humiliate other prisoners by making them sweep the streets while the natives look on. (Imperial War Museum)

The Tasik honeymoon was over. It was time to get down to learning our new trade. Just as you don't become a brain surgeon by merely signing on for the course, you don't become a competent Pow by just putting your hands up. Basic training was to start right away.

3: DOWN TO EARTH WITH THE MOKO MOKO

May - June, 1942. Surabaya and Semarang, Java

We had arrived in Tasik still white tuans, riding in comfortable trucks with out kit piled high in the back. We were to leave as coolies, on our own two feet, with everything we owned on our backs. And the Nips made it clear that anyone who found his pack too heavy would just have to abandon it and lose the lot. Packing was a harsh lesson in assessing the true value of our possessions, and of our capabilities as pack mules.

We were called out on parade long before dawn and kept standing there three hours. Not by any means a long wait by Nip standards, but useful practice for novice Pows. We spent the time torturing ourselves with speculation as to our destination. Formosa was favourite, with Nippon itself well fancied. We marched, or perhaps it would be more accurate to say staggered, past the huge flame-of-the-forest tree standing sentry at the Nip guardroom, and headed for town.

Troops with fixed bayonets lined our route. The streets were crammed with noisy crowds. Every building was festooned with Japanese flags. Our departure had been turned into a carnival, with the procession of the European slaves, presented by the glorious Nip army, as the main attraction. We were too busy preoccupied with the heat and the ever-increasing weight of our loads to pay much attention to the sightseers. We marched grimly on, striving to keep the sweat out of our eyes. Fortunately, after no more than a couple of miles we turned in at the railway station. And our train was waiting. Not a Pullman, but better than we had expected. We were thankful to pile aboard, away from those crowds, out of the sun, to ease our packs off our backs and sink on to the wooden benches.

Surprisingly the wood-fired loco clanked off almost immediately. We were on our way to goodness-knew-where with a coachful of armed Nips in the rear to keep us in order. Each time we stopped, which was frequently, the Nips leapt down on to the track and patrolled our carriages. It was quite flattering to think at least someone thought we might be tough desperadoes just waiting our chance to seize the train and made a daring getaway. All day long we rattled through fields of rice and sugar-cane. Darkness found us rolling along a high embankment, and below us, through the windows of their brightly-lit bungalows, we could see families of well-to-do Javanese gathering happily for the evening meal. We marvelled at this seeming normality in a world that for us had gone completely haywire.

Late that night, after ten hours on the move, we were turfed off the train at Surabaya, Java's second city, in the east of the island. The place was either blacked-out or the power had failed. We picked up our loads and dragged ourselves blindly through endless pitch-black streets, goaded on by guards anxious to be rid of us.

At long last we turned through a gate in a tall bamboo fence. We stumbled, still in the dark, on to a muddy square. There, weary and drenched in sweat, we were herded about while Nips counted us, recounted us and counted us again. When it was finally decided that no-one had gone off to lead a resistance movement, we were addressed by an interpreter. He impressed upon us that our sole purpose in life so long as we remained in his camp was to salute or bow to all Nip soldiers who came within range. Otherwise we would be pukuled. So we came to learn the Malay word pukul, to clout, perhaps the commonest word in the Malay-speaking Nip's vocabulary. A little more bumbling about in the dark and we were pushed and shoved into what had apparently been a school. Now every classroom, in fact every cupboard it seemed, was bulging with hungry Dutchmen. But somehow or other, after a little juggling of bodies, space was made in the corridors for us to get our heads down.

We understood why the Dutch were so hungry when we queued for breakfast next morning. We got a mess-tin of watery glue garnished with the bloated bodies of a few rice-weevil grubs. This was our introduction to what the Dutch called pap. And it was as well to get used to it, for it was the dish with which we were to start every day, with very few exceptions, until the war ended.

We gathered that the camp consisted of what had been

TELEPHONE:
Extn.
Any communications on the
subject of this letter should
be addressed to:—
THE SECRETARY,
and the following number
quoted:—

P4/FE

AIR MINISTRY,

LONDON, W.C.2.

27 *April* 1943.

747461 *Corporal D R Peacock*

Sir,

    I am directed to inform you that the position of personnel whose whereabouts have been unknown since the evacuation of the Malaya, Java and Sumatra area has been under review.

    It is regretted therefore that your *son*

must be regarded as missing with effect from 1st February, 1943.

> Just over a year after I had been taken prisoner
> the RAF posted me missing.

TELEPHONE: WORCESTER 3411
Extn.
Any communications on the
subject of this letter should
be addressed to:—
THE UNDER SECRETARY
OF STATE,
and the following number
quoted:—
YOUR REF. *Peacock*/7KCas.
747461

F.A. Form 143A.
AIR MINISTRY,

WHITTINGTON ROAD,

WORCESTER.

29·4·43.

Madam, 747461 *Cpl. D.R. Peacock*

    I have to refer with regret to the fact that your *son* has been officially reported as missing on 1.2.43 and in these circumstances you will wish to be informed with regard to the voluntary allotment of 7/- per week at present in payment to you.

    I am to state that the regulations permit of the continuance of payment at the present rate for seventeen weeks from the date the casualty was notified (i.e. four weeks as an allotment from the airman's pay, and thirteen weeks from public funds).

> With admirable efficiency they wrote again only ~~two~~
> two days later to discuss stoppng the
> 7 shillings they were paying out on my behalf

Meanwhile back at the Air Ministry…

Surabaya's Lyceum School and playground. Our arrival meant that there were now 2000 prisoners milling miserably about inside its 15 ft bamboo fences, under the watchful eyes of armed guards posted in sentry towers. There was little time to glean the full facts of life Lyceum-style before we newcomers were hustled back on to the mud square, together with all our possessions.

After keeping us hanging about long enough to emphasise what a big shot he was, our friend the interpreter appeared. First he reminded us about the importance of saluting or bowing to all Nips on the camp. It seemed our guards were so low in the pecking order that they themselves had to bow and scrape to the whole Nip army. So, not surprisingly, they were determined to make the most of the chance to humiliate someone else. There was one other order: 'Don't go within three yards of the bamboo fence'. The interpreter didn't harp on about this one. He just said we would be shot if we did.

Next came the kit inspection. We stood in line, each with all his worldly goods piled in front of him, all ready we thought for the Nips to plunder them. But, to our surprise, they didn't take much. The odd super-optimist who had hung on to a camera was quickly relieved of it. They were contraband. So too were tin helmets, which was a minor disaster because, later, helmets which survived in other camps were to prove first-class frying pans. On top of my little heap in a purposely prominent position was my diary. I thought that if I placed it under their noses the Nips would be sure to ignore it. But to my consternation an English-speaking guard picked it up and began thumbing through it. There wasn't really much chance of his reading my shorthand; it often baffles me. But I was very relieved when he gave up and tossed the book back on my heap.

Fortunately neither at this time nor at any time during my captivity did the Nips attempt to steal any money we might have. And some of us had what to the Nips must have been quite considerable sums. We had been getting paid right up to the surrender with little chance to spend it. In my case my parents, showing admirable foresight, had sent me £50 just before I left Singapore. It formed the foundation of a last-ditch emergency fund which I managed to eke out over most of my time as Pow. At last, the indignities of the kit inspection over, we were dismissed. We were now free to get together with the camp's established residents to swap experiences... and in many cases a few possessions as well.

The Dutch may have been a little short on battle cruisers and fighter planes but they had first-class mess-tins. I rate the 'blik' I bought from one of them my best buy as a prisoner apart from my coolie hat. It held twice as much as my RAF mess-tin and could be used for boiling or frying without the risk of lead poisoning. But the extra capacity certainly wasn't needed at the Lyceum. We would get two more meals a day, the Dutch told us, each consisting of a small portion of steamed rice... as distinct from the breakfast pap... and a spoonful of vegetable stew.

The only chance of supplementing what seemed to us at the time a starvation diet was to get on an outside working party where, if you were lucky, it might be possible to do a quick cash deal with a street-trader. There was tremendous competition to join these parties, particularly among the Dutch. Many of them had families living, so near and yet so far, just on the other side of the bamboo fence. Wives and children, who had not yet been interned, kept watch on the working parties from a discreet distance in the hope of exchanging a smile or a wave with the man who had been taken away from them.

The work consisted mainly of filling in air-raid shelters. The war had now passed so far on that the Nips felt they had no need of them. In any case, as they loved to point out, they, unlike us, were not afraid to die. Surprisingly I did get a trip out within a few days for my first taste of a Nip working party. Some 20 of us were loaded on to the back of a lorry and driven off through the city streets to go grass-cutting. It sounds cushy enough but there was a whole airfield to cut with small hand scythes. We had some thug-like Nip navy types as foremen. With continual shouts of "Koorah" and "Lakas" and the occasional clout or kick they made us work non-stop all day and we never got even a glimpse of a street-trader.

There was just one crumb of comfort. Working nearby were some Nip sailors who were being treated as badly, if not worse than we were. And they, we gathered, were men who had helped to rout the Allies in the Battle of the Java Sea. Unfortunately for them, however, their ship had sunk and they had failed dutifully to go down with her. For this gross misconduct, we were told, they were in disgrace and banned forever from returning home.

My next working party involved a spot of gentle excavation at what appeared to be a searchlight emplacement. Here we were introduced to the chief tool of our new trade as coolies: the chunkel, a short-handled hoe which serves as the spade of the East, and the Chinese wheelbarrow, or moko moko. The moko moko earth-and-rock shifter is a model of simplicity. It comprises a stout bamboo pole with an old sack suspended from it by two loops of sisal. It is operated simply too. Two men lug it about on their shoulders. So we scrambled down into the excavation in pairs with our poles and sacks. The Nips supervised the filling of the sacks to make sure we carried the regulation load. We then staggered, with the bamboo bruising into our shoulders and our legs buckling under the strain, up out of the hole to unload.

Sweating profusely with this unaccustomed exertion under the blazing sun we cursed the Nips under our breath and swore at our complete impotence to do anything about our plight. But we did get the occasional break, and learned what became to us the most beautiful word in the Nip language: "yasmay", meaning rest. We also contacted some of those hitherto elusive street-traders and I returned to camp triumphantly with half-a-dozen eggs and a papaya.

Those were my only two trips out of the Lyceum. For the rest of the time I was kept busy playing hide-and-seek with the camp guards. Defeated we might be, but we still felt infinitely superior to our jailers, and they knew it. They desperately needed an orgy of saluting and bowing to bolster up their ego. We could escape with a salute provided we were wearing a hat. Even this was humiliating but it was certainly preferable to bowing to them which we had to do if we were caught bareheaded. Of course we could have played the hero and tried to ignore them, but in the Lyceum it was all too easy to qualify quite unintentionally for a clout over the head with a rifle-butt, and no-one was going to invite one deliberately.

I didn't stay long enough to get to hate any of the guards personally, only to detest them in bulk for, on June 2, 200 British and 100 Dutch were rounded up and told to be ready to leave the Lyceum next day. Jimmy and I were among them. As we were now beginning to expect, we were called out on the square at 4 a.m. and kept waiting until 8 a.m. But fortunately I was quickly learning to squat patiently on my haunches like any other coolie.

At last a squad of Nip soldiers arrived at the camp to collect us. There was a lot of sharp, falsetto shouting while we went through the counting ritual to make sure no-one was being short-changed, and then off we went. We had been in that camp only 14 days: it seemed like 114.

The Lyceum had given us a sharp warning of the misery that lay ahead, but before the clouds of death and disaster were to engulf us the sun was to make one or two spectacular, if brief, break-throughs. And that incredible June 3 certainly brought one of them. Just to get outside the camp gates was a tonic itself. And there, to our surprise, we found a truck waiting to carry our heavier kit to the station. This apparently considerate attitude to us from our new jailers lightened our spirits as much as the load on our backs.

By no stretch of imagination could they have been called benevolent, but they certainly weren't half as malevolent as the bunch we had left at the Lyceum. They appeared to be ordinary soldiers, as distinct from prison guards. While they quickly made it clear they would stand no nonsense, there was none of the gratuitous shouting and clouting we had come to expect.

At the station they managed to get us aboard a train with a minimum of hassle. And this time, once we got going, there was no leaping down on to the track to guard our coaches each time we stopped. We quickly realised that here was a chance to buy from the hawkers who came walking past the train at each station with baskets of food. We gave it a try. Our Nips were much too busy guzzling themselves to worry us. We were soon all sitting back gnawing at succulent pieces of chicken. Stringy and flyblown perhaps, but to us after the Lyceum diet, as succulent as they come. It was one of the slowest of slow trains, but we were in no hurry. We began to appreciate that the bloke who wrote that it is better to travel than to arrive, or words to that effect, may well have had something. So far as we were concerned the journey could have gone on forever. But mid-afternoon found us crawling into a large town which the Dutch who were with us said was Semarang, situated about midway along Java's north coast.

The clanging and general hubbub of the train's arrival had long died away before we were allowed to clamber down on to the platform of a gloomy and strangely silent station. As we were marched off we became aware that the area had been completely cleared of all civilians.

Then, as we emerged from the shadows into the brilliant sunshine outside, a terrific clamour burst upon our ears and a fantastic sight dazzled our eyes. The whole station approach was crammed with Dutch women, gay in brightly coloured frocks and all cheering wildly.

They surged towards us, and while yelling, sweating Nips strove hopelessly to keep some sort of order, money, soap and chocolate were pressed into our hands. Somehow these women had discovered that a trainload of prisoners was due and, although faced with terrible problems themselves, had turned out in their hundreds to give us a welcome more suited to conquering heroes than to a bunch of defeated demoralised Pows.

Eventually the Nips began to win the battle to keep the women back. We were herded into a little park near the station. The women were penned in on the surrounding footpaths. But they weren't beaten. As we went through the counting and recounting routine, before being taken over by a new set of Nips, it simply rained sweets and cigarettes tossed by our new friends. The effect of such an amazing out-of-this-world reception was electric. We moved off whistling and singing, with the women cheering us on.

Of course the women had come mainly in the hope of seeing some of their own menfolk, but when the 100 Dutch prisoners were marched off in a different direction many of the girls continued to run gaily alongside our party. Everyone was enjoying the show, except the Nips. They finally moved in to break up the party when the women joined us with tremendous enthusiasm in a rousing chorus of "There'll Always Be An England".

A couple of miles farther on, when the Nips stopped us for a breather, the girls began gathering again. But the Nip commander had had more than enough. He ordered his men to fix bayonets and called in reinforcements in the shape of the Javanese police to help to keep the women away.

When we marched off again one or two brave spirits still tried to keep contact with us. One of them, a boy on a bike, seemed determined to follow us to our destination. Sadly we had to look on helplessly while he was kicked and beaten up by a Nip guard.

Soon the town was left behind, but still we trudged on, now along a dead straight road across a swampy plain. At long last we turned in at a large tumbledown house standing in a clump of trees. We judged by the entanglement of shiny new barbed wire that we were expected. And indeed the long-deserted rooms had been filled up with wooden sleeping platforms on trestles, and in the garden a Nip-style field kitchen had been erected. And the day's miracles were not yet over. As we prepared to doss down, a lorry rumbled in with an amazing load of luxury... mattresses, apparently commandeered from a former Dutch army barracks. Astonishingly we seemed to have stumbled across a Nip CO who actually believed in some sort of comfort for prisoners.

There was just one cloud at the end of the this sunny day: a cloud of ferocious Semarang mosquitoes. And our precious mosquito nets had been left behind with the kit we had last seen in Surabaya. So, ironically, the night that those mattresses should have given us our best sleep for weeks was spent lashing around at the bloodsuckers that were trying to gorge themselves on our bodies. Those who did fall asleep had badly bitten faces, arms and legs next day to prove it.

4: NIGHT OF THE STINK BEETLES

June - July, 1942. Semarang Aerodrome, Java

Dawn and pap with the inevitable fat weevil grubs finally wiped out our exuberance of the day before. We scarcely had time to get the revolting mess down before we were dragged out to continue our march along the straight flat road.

This time we hadn't far to go. After no more than a mile or so we were herded on to Kalibantan aerodrome where, waiting for us on their track were three trains of sand and a squad of Nips poised to ensure their rapid unloading. But it wasn't going to be as easy as all that. The idea of walking around carrying a couple of shovelfuls of sand in a little cockleshell-shaped basket didn't fire our enthusiasm. It seemed an incredibly stupid way of doing the job. And, of course, there was the sheer indignity of it. The transformation from European to coolie was going to take just a little time.

At first the Nips, who didn't seem to have much idea themselves of what they were about, proved fairly passive but, as the morning wore on without much appreciable progress, they became increasingly restive. It was not a moment too soon when, around noon, a couple of our cookhouse-wallahs came jogging along the road in the fore and aft shafts of a wheelless wheelbarrow, carrying a load of nasi goreng, fried rice. The Nips called a truce. We threw away those wretched baskets and ran off to witness the meticulous sharing out of the meal. Satisfied that each had got his share, and no more, we wolfed it down. You didn't even notice the weevil grubs when they were mixed up with the veg and odd bits of meat in the fried rice.

After the break, with the tropical sun now blazing hot, work became even slower. We couldn't see that there was a hope in hell of our unloading the three trains that day. But the Nips had been ordered to get the job done, and done it had to be. Their first solution to the problem was to have more men up in the wagons filling the baskets. As a result the fillers got in one another's way and work became even slower. The Nips sent in more men, and brought the job to a standstill. They then went berserk, beating or kicking any prisoner within reach. It was a long, grim, bruising afternoon. But, realising that we were there until the job was finished, we got on with it despite the Nips. And some little while after dark all the wagons were pronounced empty and every grain of sand deposited in its appointed place.

It was marvellous just to stop work. And a billet free of Lyceum-style bull was something to be grateful for too. We dowsed ourselves in deliciously cold tap water and knocked back a palatable rice-and-stew supper. Our missing kit had arrived during the day, and we were quickly under our nets safe from the wretched mozzies, enjoying those miraculous mattresses.

The Dutch had built Kalibantan aerodrome on the coastal marshes. A purely civil airport with a short runway was apparently a dead loss so far as the Nips were concerned, so they planned to turn it into something really useful with a runway running far enough out into the swamps to take their bombers. They had brought us in to do the coolie work. We seemed to have lost our prisoner-of-war status and become a slave-labour battalion attached to the Nip army. Nominally in charge of the transformation of Kalibantan were two Dutch civil engineers. We didn't question too seriously why they were working for the enemy. For although they strolled around looking very important in their brilliant white shirts and shorts and topees, they were very frightened men.

They dared not openly show any friendship towards us, but passed on a few words of encouragement when they were sure the Nips were not watching. They were prisoners too, in all but name, though they were paroled each night to go home to their wives.

The real boss so far as we were concerned (and we were the whole labour force apart from a handful of Javanese recruited for the more skilled jobs) was a gnome-like Nip with an over-size sun helmet which gave him a sort of animated toadstool look. Looking back I suppose he was not a bad sort so far as Nips went, but obviously there were communication difficulties, and he was not over-endowed with patience. When he smiled and bared his more than adequate set of gold-filled teeth all was well. When he danced up and down with rage it was prudent to keep your distance, particularly if he had any sort of weapon to hand. He was the first Nip we got to know on personal cussing terms. Obviously he had to have a name for us to attach our adjectives to. Naturally he became Goldie. From the very first day Goldie and his terror squad made sure we earned our tenancy of those mattresses.

Industrial relations did improve a little when, in a giant technological leap forward, the hated baskets were replaced by a light railway. We now loaded the sand direct from the wagons into skips, which we pushed out along our new rails to the runway workings. Much more dignified labour this: it raised us to the status of pit ponies. But the increased productivity didn't mean that the Nips could step up the number of sand trains and throw in a few loads of clay and rocks for good measure. And, of course, as we progressed, the unloading site got farther and farther away.

We soon found there was absolutely no point in obstructing the work or going slow. The Nips set us a quota for each day, and if it was not completed at knocking–off time they simply kept us working until it was. For their part, they gradually realised that the less they tried to organise us the quicker we finished the job.

One of the Semarang 200 found his old hut still standing when he made a sentimental journey back to the aerodrome in 1977. The bamboo sides had been replaced with corrugated iron but the roof and projecting steel struts remained unchanged. (Martin Ofield)

By their own standards, I'm sure the Semarang Nips treated us reasonably well, but those standards left a great deal to be desired. Any reluctance to obey an order, real or merely imagined by the Nips, brought an instant beating. Mostly it was a matter of slaps, punches and kicks, but occasionally they got really tough.

Many incidents arose from misunderstandings. For instance, when a Nip held out an arm stiffly in my direction and began flapping his hand at me I reckoned that to anyone but an idiot this must mean "Go away." I then learned rather painfully that to the Nip it meant "Come here." A more serious misunderstanding earned one of our officers, a flight-lieutenant, a cut on the head from the flat edge of Goldie's bayonet which required several stitches and some days off work before he came up smiling for more. His mistake was that he thought that prisoners had rights, the right in this case to sufficient time to eat their midday rice.

We had five officers with us at Semarang: the C.O. who was the wing commander of the puce face from Tasikmalaya, an M.O., and three spares. The spares went out with the working party, as junior foremen when things were going well, and Aunt Sallies when the Nips became fractious. On June 16 we clocked up our hundredth day as prisoners. The Rice Legend prophecy, like the padre's hint of help from the hills, had come to nought. To keep up our spirits we fell back on wild, totally false rumours of Allied troops poised to rescue us. Though why we thought ourselves worth rescuing I can't imagine.

I almost enjoyed the morning march to work. The road ran along a causeway raised above the rice fields and swamps, often blanketed at this time of day in a thick low-lying mist. Here and there a ghostly movement in the paddies would manifest itself as a young Javanese riding a water buffalo. On the road itself on market days we passed natives driving lazily along in heavy carts pulled by drowsy bullocks, and others jogging along on foot with their wares swinging from either end of the pikulan, the bamboo pole across their shoulders.

And away in the distance the rising sun floodlit the spine of Java floating above the mists. In the clear morning air we could make out every nook and cranny of the mountains of Ungaran and Prahu and the volcanoes of Sumbing and Sundoro. They appeared just up the road, but as the day progressed they would gradually clothe themselves in an ever-thickening veil of cloud and then finally vanish altogether.

But our morning walks didn't last long. On June 28 we found ourselves suddenly uprooted from our country mansion and installed in huts on the airfield. We made the move in a mood of wild optimism. On the three previous nights there had been air-raid warnings; now a hurried and totally unexpected switch to a more secure billet. Who could doubt the significance of these two events? More rational minds might have concluded that they were totally unconnected. The Nips had decided to test their air-raid sirens and around the same time it had occurred to them that it was foolish to have their coolies wasting time walking to work when they could easily be accommodated on the job. But we needed good rumours to keep us going. So we decided it could all add up to only one thing: the Allies were on their way.

Meanwhile, while we were waiting, blissfully unaware of the sort of conditions we should face in the long years ahead, we grumbled about our new ramshackle billets with their bamboo sleeping-shelves. A few square feet of bamboo turned out to be the standard accommodation Pows-for-use-of throughout Indonesia and Malaya. It served as bedroom, dining room, lounge, the lot. As we sat there that first night eating our evening rice we looked like nothing so much as a row of battery hens on their perches. But I soon came to regard my bit of shelf as my only refuge in a cruel world, finding it bliss to get my head down there after a bruising day on working party. The bamboo quickly became 'home'.

There was one essential missing from our new camp. It had no fence. And no self-respecting Pow wants to be in a camp without proper security. The Nips, perhaps appreciating our feelings, chucked us a few rolls of barbed wire and told us to cage ourselves in. The barbed wire may have kept us in, but it couldn't keep unwelcome visitors out. They came in their hundreds of thousands on the Night of the Stink Beetles. These dirty grey round insects blanketed the mosquito nets like swarming bees. Outside a solid column of swirling insects stretched five feet down from the light above the camp entrance. They were everywhere. Killing them seemed like blowing against the wind. Worse in fact, because only when crushed did they give off their incredibly foul smell. Fortunately they vanished as suddenly as they had arrived, and the next night the field was left open to the mosquitoes homing in from the surrounding swamp, patrolling our nets to strike at anyone careless enough to offer them a target.

Rumours dried up. There was nothing to break the dreary monotony of unloading and spreading sand, until, on July 7, to our complete surprise, a hundred Dutchmen joined us on the camp. They were the party who had parted from us at Semarang station after the journey from Surabaya. Their arrival caused a great stir in itself, but next morning we were left gawping in amazement as their wives, families and friends turned up at the camp gates and were actually allowed in to see them. Even more fantastic still, we heard that there were more women at the Nip guardroom laden with food and demanding to see the British.

This caught the Nips on the hop. Obviously someone at very high level had granted permission for the Dutch prisoners to receive their families. Equally obviously the order did not include the British. There could be only one answer: no orders, no visitors. Goldie turned out the guard to put an end to the matter. We had been as astounded as the Nips at our friends' arrival. Never in our wildest dreams had we imagined any such visit possible. We were deeply touched by the gesture, but amazed that anyone should ever have thought that it could succeed. We resignedly prepared to go to the sand trains.

But we had grossly underestimated the Ladies of Semarang. They had risen early, loaded up bikes with whatever food they could lay hands on and cycled in the heat all the way from town. They were not to be so easily dismissed by Goldie and his goons. They stood their ground, demanded, and eventually obtained permission to see the Nip C.O. Presumably the Emperor's Rules and Regulations does not say very much about coping with persistent women demanding to be allowed to bring cheer to prisoners. The C.O. argued loud and long but eventually despairingly gave in. The girls poured through the camp gates. The Pows' Picnic was on.

These indomitable women, with their menfolk imprisoned, facing rocketing prices with dwindling savings, with their very lives on a knife-edge, had still found the time, the energy, the cash, to say nothing of the courage to give us our one happy day as Nip prisoners. Perhaps if the Nips had had to face in battle the Ladies of Semarang, instead of mere Dutch and British troops, Java would never have fallen. They showered us with gifts. We sat, feasted, smoked, and, above all, enjoyed the close proximity of clean, fresh, scented bodies. It wasn't that so many of us were pining for women. The long hours of hard manual labour on a miserable diet left us too drained to think very often of much else than food, rest and when the whole ghastly nightmare was going to end. But it was wonderful to experience this tantalising reminder that there were other things in life.

Like us, the women were living on hopes. They believed that the Nip avalanche which had engulfed their islands had been halted. They were impatiently waiting for some sign of Allied advances. They were even looking to the Javanese, who had now discovered that 'Asia for the Asiatics' really meant 'Asia for the Nips', to help end their ordeal. Fortunately neither they nor we yet realised that we still hadn't really begun to learn what capture by the Nips meant.

We enjoyed our happy hour, then collected and pooled the left-overs. So lavish had our visitors been that we each received a handout of 100 cigarettes, and some fruitcake and sweets, and our cookhouse was enriched with tea, coffee and even some butter.

If the Nips believed that the day they showed a human face was going to help productivity, they were sadly disappointed next morning. The picnic had reawakened us to what we were missing, re-focussed fading memories of life way back at home. The zombie-like work rhythm we had adopted was shattered. And though we had a hundred Dutchmen to help us and only one extra train to unload, we soon fell way behind schedule. The exasperated Nips turned nasty. Roughings-up became savage and frequent. And they continued on throughout the day, slowing rather than quickening the pace. Eventually pitch darkness made it impossible to carry on. For once we had failed to finish the job.

As we returned sullenly to our huts the angry Nips warned us that the next day, on top of our usual quota of trains, we would have not only the backlog to shift, but also four extra trains of sand and two of stone. And this time the whole lot would be cleared no matter what.

I lined up next morning dreading the day's work. But the only thing certain about life as a Nip Pow was that you could never be certain of anything. Before the column moved off for the runway, the Nips cut out 20 men. I was one of them. We were ordered up on the back of a lorry. We were driven out of camp wondering what terrible job had been lined up for us but feeling that this time, at any rate, it couldn't be much worse than the sand trains.

As we headed up into the hills we overtook large numbers of

Nip cycle troops, sweating profusely as they pedalled furiously along in full battle kit. Then we came upon artillery units and infantry. The hills were simply crawling with Nips. Deep down we'd never really swallowed the rumours of imminent invasion, for lack of concrete evidence to back them up. But then we knew little evidence against them either. And just what could all these troops be doing here anyway? We joked about being human shields for advancing troops, or providing the ultimate in realistic targets for snipers. But beneath all the banter we became uneasy. Suddenly work on the runway didn't seem so bad after all.

Our lorry halted a moment while a six-man gun team on the road in front of us took their weapon to pieces and then hared up a cliff carrying the bits on their backs. The road deteriorated into a rough track, but on we went, higher and higher. We now reached remote scrubland: just the place for a quiet execution. The lorry stopped on the crest of a hill, and we were ordered to get off.

The Nips split us up into groups of four and distributed us among infantry squads dug in along a ridge commanding the

Sweat towels at the ready, a Nip gun team marches to war. The hills were crawling with Nips like those in this Imperial War Museum picture when Don Peacock joined them on manoeuvres

41

whole of the surrounding area. The soldiers in the dug-out where my group found ourselves seemed reasonably relaxed. Not really in the mood, we thought, for bayonetting us or anyone else.

It dawned on us gradually that some Nip commander with a bizarre sense of humour had brought us along to add a little realism to his army manoeuvres. We had been conscripted into the force defending the ridge. It was a sort of replay of a battle that never was. The Dutch had chosen this site and dug the trenches for a stand against the invaders, but surrendered instead. Now we had to defend the ridge against the Nips. Our new commanding officer had drawn the line at carrying realism too far. So for weapons we were given tin cans to beat, flags to wave, and clay to throw when we spotted the enemy coming up the hill. All good clean fun really. We saw them in the distance, well out of tin-can range, all decked out in twigs, leaves and grass. Then they vanished. For twenty minutes we stood, tins at the ready, on the alert for the attack, but nothing stirred.

Then suddenly a group leapt out of the undergrowth at our feet. I rattled away on my tin, arguably my most belligerent act of the war in the Pacific. We were facing up to the onslaught with, I thought, great heroism, when another bunch of Nips cowardly attacked us from the rear. We were done for. It was just a matter of how many enemy we could account for with our clay before we were annihilated. One over-enthusiastic Pow scored two powerful direct hits on an enemy officer. He dropped dead in true cowboys-and-Indians style. But one of our own Nips, enraged at such insubordination, and apparently forgetting which side he was on, immediately laid into the Pow. At this, fortunately, the dead officer quickly came back to life and jumped to his feet just in time to stop a savage beating. Soon we were all declared officially killed, a privileged category which allowed us to relax, lie on our backs and drink in the cool mountain air while all around us the Nip crazy gang went on careering up and down the hills toting machine-guns, trench mortars and field guns. We had time to contemplate that perhaps there was one thing worse than being a Nip Pow, and that was being a Nip soldier.

Even after the battle was over and we were on our way back to camp in our comfortable lorry, a gun team came galloping down the road, not only pulling their gun but carrying ammo packs and huge hammers on their back as well. They came smartly to a halt, swung their gun and gear on to a lorry and snapped to attention. A passing officer, obviously not quite so impressed as we were, immediately slapped their faces one by one. A little farther along the road another group of soldiers seemed to be having no better luck with an officer who was minutely inspecting their bikes.

After this day of farce we settled down for a while to a fairly calm humdrum sort of existence. We ate our pap each morning and marched off to the runway. We unloaded our wagons of sand, clay and rocks, shoved skips along the tracks and looked busy. We had developed the art of looking industrious even when we were doing nothing because it kept the Nips happy. And a happy Nip was a harmless Nip. We had a yasmay about mid morning, stopped again for our nasi goreng about midday and for another yasmay in the afternoon. All the while our drinking water bubbled hygienically in a couple of old petrol drums set up over wood fires.

Looking after the water (a job I very much fancied but never managed to get) was Johnny. Johnny was a fastidious sort of chap. He didn't use the bamboo drinking-tubes like everybody else, but kept his old cracked enamel mug beside the petrol drums with a drink cooling in it. We all respected Johnny's mug and no-one ever dreamed of using it. No-one, that is, until one yasmay when a stray Nip came up and took a sip from it while Johnny was distracted, talking to friends.

But this liberty didn't go unnoticed. The incensed Johnny came storming across to snatch up the defiled mug. He pointedly moved off to place it out of reach of further intruders. Then it was the Nip's turn to feel insulted. He called Johnny back and lined an almighty blow at Johnny's head. But he wasn't quite quick enough. Johnny ducked and the fist landed with a resounding thwack across the face of another astonished Nip who had turned up for a drink. For a moment all three participants in this slapstick routine looked at one another thunderstruck. Johnny recovered first and set off like a rocket with the first Nip in hot pursuit. They completed their first circuit of the airfield at an electrifying speed. The outer guard, patrolling with rifles balanced lazily over their shoulders, grinned and remained neutral. The pace slackened noticeably second time round, and eventually the Nip, his rage apparently burned out by his exertions, gave up the chase, and Johnny returned to his water drums miraculously unscathed.

Life at this time was good by Pow standards. In the evenings as we marched back to our huts we even broke out into song. "Bluebirds over...pause... the White Cliffs of Dover" echoed mournfully across the malarial swamp where Javanese were collecting fish they had trapped in flooded fields by shutting the gates just before the tide went out.

Our performances, including the usual Services bawdy specials, would not perhaps have had the discerning concertgoer in ecstasy, but we had our fan club: the Nips. As we belted out "That's My Girl Salome" surly thugs were turned into happy sandboys. They jogged along beside us beaming with delight and enthusiastically called for an encore whenever we showed signs of flagging. So apparent was their joy in our recitals that on days when we felt they had been too free with their rifle butts we stopped their evening treat as punishment and returned to camp in sullen silence. Perhaps, looking back, we were being cruel, because this was about all the poor devils seemed to get in the way of entertainment.

We were now well into the long dry season. It was hell slaving out on the runway under the blazing hot sun, but the cloudless nights had a certain magic. We often sat out for a while after supper under brilliant stars that seemed twice the size of those at home and discussed the same old topic: food.

Life was not all unrelieved misery. Once we accepted that we really had become coolies we were able to adjust our expectations to our new rôle in life. Although we drooled constantly about such delights we didn't really expect roast beef and Yorkshire pud for dinner any more than we had expected larks' tongues for supper in the Naafi.

So we weren't often disappointed. In fact, fewer weevil grubs in the morning pap or definite traces of water buffalo in the evening stew gave us considerable pleasure. Even just relaxing our bodies on the bamboo after a gruelling day produced something approaching enjoyment. And when, after three solid weeks of being kicked up and down the runway, we were given a day off, it seemed something like bliss. Indeed the camp looked quite festive with drying shorts, shirts and assorted rags flying from every available inch of barbed wire.

We even found time for a spot of first aid for our tattered clothing. One or two of us still had our "housewives," the little bundles of cotton, wool, tin buttons and needles thoughtfully provided by the RAF. I had always suspected that they had been invented by some fiendish brasshat largely as an extra item to be found missing at kit inspections, but ours at least we put to practical use.

The camp guards also seemed in holiday mood. They had caught three scorpions and amused themselves by ringing their captives with blazing petrol and crowding round to watch them commit seppuku. This little fiesta may have been quite a red-letter day but shortly afterwards another event really knocked us back on our heels. The impossible happened: we had a pay day.

One of the ground rules for keeping sane as a prisoner was never to believe a word the Nips said. So when earlier they had announced that we were to be paid for our labour we had simply ignored them. They were merely adding lies to brutality, we thought, in their efforts to get more work out of us. But one evening we arrived back behind the barbed wire to be told that the Nips had actually handed over ten cents for each day each man had worked during June. As ten cents worked out at about a penny, it was scarcely lavish payment, but a penny a day is not a bad percentage increase on nothing. And for many of us cash was rapidly running out.

For some time, as work stopped for the midday rice, Javanese entrepreneurs had been materialising out of the swamp and laying out their merchandise at the end of the runway. The Nips had never authorised this minimarket but they used it themselves and generally turned a blind eye if a prisoner made a purchase. Now everyone had some money and was eager to spend it. So for a couple of days we marched back to camp with mess-tins stuffed with coffee, palm sugar, bananas and the local bread. Our evening meal became a banquet, but not long enough for us to get too worried about over-eating.

What did ruffle the calm of our little world at this time was the arrival of a Nip who was not only vicious but quite obviously insane. Worse still, his officers seemed to consider that insanity excused everything, and let him do whatever he liked. As he seemed to have no specific duties we generally managed to keep well out of his way, but the odd Javanese who was unlucky enough to cross his path was cruelly beaten up, while the rest of the Nips looked on quite unconcerned. This madman somehow acquired a monkey which he took to the runway with him each day. He amused himself by beating the wretched animal with a stick, swinging it around by its tail and, for an encore, burying it in the sand. Our sympathy for the monkey was tempered by the thought that if his master hadn't been preoccupied in this fashion he might well have been tormenting one of us. And we feared he could well get away with murder.

Meanwhile we had another problem. Right from our arrival in Semarang the mosquitoes had been unfriendly. Now they showed just what a menace they could be. Soon 56 of the 200 British were on their bamboos with malaria at the same time. While my fighting qualities generally showed a great deal to be desired, I carried on my personal war against the mozzies with commendable vigour. I can claim with reasonable certainty that not one invaded my net and lived. But they got me just the same. I had a habit of putting my right hand behind my head while asleep. One night it must have touched the net. That was target enough for the Semarang mozzies. They could bite through thick khaki drill, let alone flimsy netting. Next morning I awoke with a tell-tale line of wart-like bumps across my knuckle.

Shortly afterwards I was overtaken by a sort of giddy drunkenness while on the runway. Somehow I got through the day and back to camp. Nothing seemed quite real (not an entirely unpleasant feeling for a Pow) but soon came a soaring temperature and violent headache. I lay on my bamboo completely detached from my surroundings, caring nothing for anything or anyone. Not even feeling hungry. Next came the sweating. I could have wrung water out of my bedding had I had the strength.

Malaria affected some chaps in odd ways. One climbed out of his mosquito net at 3 a.m., draped his blanket around him, and set off, he explained later, to ask the Nip commandant to send him back to England. The guard on the gate just stared at the strange apparition in astonishment and let him walk out unchallenged. However, on reaching the Nip quarters it somehow dawned on the ghost that perhaps 3 a.m. was not the ideal time to pay a call, and he padded quietly back past the guard and returned to his bamboo.

I hadn't the strength for sleep-walking. I felt worse than I had ever felt in my life. But fortunately malaria was the one disease our MO had the means to treat. Pre-war Java had been the world's chief source of quinine. And now, with the bulk of the market cut off, the Nips had such a surfeit of the stuff that they were even prepared to dole out some for Pows. Maybe we didn't get the sugary sweets we were familiar with – more like bits of dehydrated putty – but the dirty, grey, bitter pellets were no less effective, and, contrary to my forebodings, I recovered.

As well as the mozzies, flies were becoming a serious nuisance. They swarmed around anything remotely resembling food. It was impossible to keep them off our plates as we ate. They clung to the rice on our forks as we lifted it to our mouths. We couldn't avoid occasionally eating them. Perhaps they provided a little much-needed protein. These pests bred in their hundreds of thousands in the latrine trench. And with nothing to spray them or their maggots there was little we could do to fight them.

By the end of July there was an absentee on the runway. The mad Nip's monkey had disappeared. His comrades said he had taken it to the top of the airfield's control tower and dropped it off.

5: GUESTS OF THE EMPEROR

August, 1942 - February, 1943. Semarang, Java

August was a crazy month. We became so drunk on wild rumour that if someone had suggested that Snow White and her seven dwarfs were ploughing through the Java Sea in a yellow submarine to snatch us to freedom, I feel that at least some of us would have listened. How the torrent of totally unfounded reports began I cannot imagine. But, hungry as we were for any scrap of good news, we eagerly swallowed one phoney story after another. Even when the saintly Ladies of Semarang turned up at the camp gates only to be roughly turned away, we found new hope in our disappointment. It could only be that the Nips were reacting to the disastrous war news we fondly believed they were receiving.

A series of air-raid warnings, two in daylight, further fired our imagination. Then one night, as we sat under the stars swapping even more rumours, we saw a green rocket arc over the mountains. Someone recalled the padre's Easter Day text, "I will lift up mine eyes unto the hills, from whence cometh my help." Perhaps the Good Book had something after all. And before long we were deciding that the British, the Dutch, the Yanks, and perhaps even the Chinese had landed on our island.

A couple of days later came the confirmation we needed. One of our cooks, taken to Semarang by the Nips to collect some veg, came back swearing that they had passed a convoy of Nip lorries loaded with corpses, followed by more trucks carrying wounded. This was it. Our self-deception grew to such a pitch that one or two of my more resourceful friends collected fishplates from our light railway, smuggled them into camp and sharpened them up to use as weapons. And on the afternoon of August 16, when the Nips suddenly stopped us working and hurried us back behind the camp barbed wire, we were ready for anything; well, more or less anything. The Nips seemed disorganised. We noted with special interest that some of the guard-posts were no longer manned. We assumed that many of the camp Nips had been called away to help stem the Allied advance. It was time to start planning the gargantuan feasts we would have immediately we reached home.

We waited impatiently, but day followed day without any sign of imminent release. The air-raid warnings ceased. The missing guards returned to their posts. Work on the runway was resumed with a vengeance. And on August 30 we quietly clocked up our 176th day in the bag and cancelled our homecoming banquets. Whether the Nips had been indulging in some massive exercise, or whether we had just dreamed up the whole thing, we never knew.

There were still rumours. There were always rumours. But now they centred on remote Pacific islands, most of which we'd never even heard of.

The Nips were their usual charming selves again, all except one. This weird character, showing a touching concern for our welfare, came into the huts one morning and amazed us by insisting that we all collect our bedding (or what passed for bedding) and put it outside on the grass to air. No sense in catching a chill.

Then there was Al Capone, a morose individual who was very proud of his smattering of English, somewhat basic but reasonably recognisable, that he had picked up on Yokohama docks. He often spent yasmay periods showing off his linguistic skill, and indeed endeavouring to improve it. He even went so far as to strike up something akin to friendship with a prisoner. Their exchanges were limited but they tried to talk about their homes and civvy jobs. Al produced a photo of his wife and three children, which came as a shock as many of us at that time found it difficult to accept that Nips were human enough to have families. The ill-starred association predictably came to a sudden and violent end. Al knew all too well the meaning of "bastard", perhaps having been frequently called one by sailors visiting ships in the bad old days before the Nips had put the white man in his proper place. What he didn't realise was that, among servicemen at anyrate, context and tone of voice can turn the word from an insult to almost a term of endearment. One afternoon he heard his English friend, defending their get-togethers in a verbal brawl with critical comrades, refer to Al, as "not a bad old bastard." At this he flew into a rage, laid into his friend, and showed what an evil young bastard he really could be.

A few days later a Nip with a rather refined English vocabulary (in fact a genuine Westernised Oriental Gentleman) literally dropped in on us. Up to this time the Nips had been using Semarang Aerodrome as little more than a railway siding. But late one afternoon our aching limbs and bored minds were given a little respite when work was halted to allow three light aircraft to land on our runway. And to our astonishment, as we resumed our labours, the pilot of one of them came strolling over towards us. After all the recent rumours it did cross my mind that he might be coming over to surrender to us. But no, he was, apparently, impelled by solicitous concern for our welfare.

He was, he claimed in Oxford English, appalled at the standard of hospitality we were receiving from his country. He assured us that this deplorable state of affairs would soon be remedied. When someone mentioned the word 'prisoners', our knight in shining armour quickly corrected him. We were not prisoners, he said, but guests of the Emperor. Well, the Emperor's guests were now so hungry that the chief topics of conversation as we pushed our loads of sand and rocks around the runway were vitamins and proteins, and, among the more pragmatic, just how long we could survive if we didn't soon get adequate supplies of both of them.

Our restricted diet was beginning to have its effects. We had adapted ourselves extraordinarily well to coolie life. A few unfortunates with sensitive skins were obliged to go around looking like music hall Bedouins, but for the most part our bodies stood the long days almost naked in the fierce sun without apparent ill effect. Sadly, however, in some cases our eyes couldn't. The MO had no difficulty in diagnosing the trouble. He told the increasing number of men who could no longer stand the blinding heat that their plight was due to vitamin deficiency. But, with little in his medicine chest except quinine, there was not much he could do about it. One of the worst affected was a new friend, a Londoner called Bert, one of the many who had walked straight off the ship from Blighty into a prison camp. Of course the MO had no cure, but he wasn't entirely beaten. From somewhere or other he rustled up a piece of cardboard (an extremely a rare commodity itself) and from it produced a mask with protruding eye-slots. Bert did his stint on the runway looking like something left over from a science-fiction film set, but it made his life just a little more bearable. He never complained much, though he must have been terrified to find his eyesight failing with not a hope in hell of getting the treatment he needed. No one laughed at my coolie hat any more.

My cash was dwindling and the Nips seemed to have over-looked our ten cents a day for July and August, but I still managed to buy the occasional banana or papaya from the natives at the end of the runway. I was now vitamin-conscious enough to believe that any cash that added fresh fruit to my diet was cash well spent. In fact, as the future we were saving our emergency funds for was looking more and more doubtful, Jim, Bert and I treated ourselves to the absolute luxury of an egg apiece which we fried in some similarly expensive coconut oil. We were in need of a little extra cheer as the long dry season was drawing to a close and our atap thatch had failed its first test against a genuine torrential down-pour. And then, as we huddled together, wet, cold and miserable, our last lingering illusions that the island was under imminent threat of attack was shattered by the news that the Nips were to instal floodlights for nightwork. Even the most optimistic among us had to admit that, so far from invasion, this suggested that there were no Allied forces near enough to mount even an occasional night air raid.

We had now completed the foundations of the runway exten-sion and the Nips were eager to push ahead with surfacing it. There were obviously going to be big changes in our work routine, and change didn't generally mean an improvement.

In the event the new rota was nothing like as bad as we had feared. The day was divided into three shifts: 8 a.m. to 1 p.m., 2 p.m. to 5.30 p.m. and a half strength 6.30 p.m. to 11 p.m. session. The work force was split into three groups, each group working two shifts for two days and only one on the third. More impor-tant, there were bribes: a tomato, a cucumber, and, unheard-of luxury, a tiny loaf of coarse bread waiting for each man when he completed a night shift. What more could a Pow ask?

There was even a nostalgic touch in the shape of some cement-mixers bearing the then-familiar name of Winget. We didn't suppose that the Nips had had them brought in specially to make us feel at home, but we were glad to see them. They were concrete proof that Britain really did exist and that our old lives were not just a figment of our imagination. Mind you, the Nips didn't treat cement-mixers much better than they treated Pows. The machines were fed on boiling tar and granite chippings. Our

51

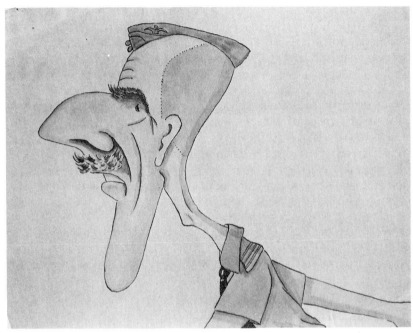

Wing-Commander in Wellies. Another old Semarangian, Ron Thompson, still treasures this sketch of Wing-Commander Gregson, drawn by a fellow-prisoner in 1943. The wing commander was the officer whose bark kept us in line when Nip warplanes buzzed our parade at Tasikmalaya after the surrender. He was still barking (at the Nips) when senior officer at Semarang

job was to pour the resultant black sago into wheelbarrows and wheel it into the path of a steamroller.

At first the arrangements worked well from our point of view, particularly as the night-shift supper appeared regularly. But inevitably there was a snag. The Nips did not dole out their little loaves of bread for nothing. They expected some extremely hard graft in return. It soon became clear that they had been given a completion deadline from on high, a deadline that they dared not fail to keep. They began putting on pressure in the only way they knew: constant beatings. A bruising time was had by all. It all built up to a final frenzied effort on October 7. With all hands working all three shifts we completed the tarring and gave the whole job a professional touch with a coat of fine gravel. We would have had reason to be proud of our achievement had we done it for the right side.

However, whomever we were working for, we certainly expected a day or two off after our efforts, and were very disgruntled next morning when we were marched out to work as usual. It seemed we had not quite achieved perfection. That fine gravel finish was not find enough.

The Nips lined up 150 of us across one end of the runway then drove us forward at snail pace encouraging us in their usual way to pick up any piece of gravel adjudged too large, an offending bit of straw here, a stray twig there. These blemishes removed, our masterpiece was beautiful to behold. But were our bosses happy? They were not. They gave us each a brush of twigs and herded us down their precious runway again, this time walking backwards, carefully grooming the surface as we went. Perfection at last. Not a speck of gravel out of place.

Then came disaster in the shape of a Javanese ice-cream seller. He had somehow arrived on the scene unnoticed, and was apparently quite oblivious to the fact that a great work of art was spread out all around him.

Before anyone could stop him, he had strolled diagonally right across the hallowed ground, leaving a trail of ugly footsteps in his wake.

The habitual bawling of the guards and grumbling of the prisoners hushed abruptly. The Nips stood transfixed at the enormity of the crime. Surely for them the earth ceased turning on its axis.

Then the storm of anger broke. Howls of anguish rent the sweaty air. The unfortunate ice-cream seller, seized by the hair, went down under a hail of blows from Nip fists and rifle-butts. As he lay on the ground he was kicked mercilessly. Meanwhile another Nip danced up and down on the vacuum box containing the ice-cream. When justice Tokyo-style had been done, the Nips gloomily surveyed the scarred runway. One made a desultory attempt to smooth out the damage with his boots. But it was apparent that there was only one possible solution. We picked up our twig brushes and lined up backwards to begin the big sweep all over again. And this time the sacred gravel remained unsullied. There was not a Javanese, ice-cream seller or otherwise, within miles.

However any hope that we could now get back to our huts for a little quiet relaxation on the bamboo was quickly dashed by the arrival of trucks loaded with barrels of waste oil, and an indication from the Nips that they would be obliged if we would be so good as to roll the barrels out into the surrounding swamp and stack them in piles. Nothing the Nips did surprised us any more, but we were curious about the barrels until it was explained to us that we were to be treated to a grand air spectacular by the all-conquering Nipponese air force the very next day. The barrels were presumably meant to represent the US Navy.

We managed to get back behind our barbed wire by mid-afternoon and at last got our heads on our bamboo. But still there was to be little peace. In no time at all, it seemed, guards came running excitedly into our huts to chase us out for a parade.

We found that during our catnap an astonishing transformation had taken place around us. The usually deserted airfield was now a mass of cars and troops. Nip officers scurried hither and thither holding their long curved swords to their sides (presumably to avoid tripping themselves up) as they struggled valiantly to restore some sort of order out of the general chaos. We were surprised to see Nip soldiers, generally a scruffy mob, putting on the bull as though they were the Coldstream Guards.

Just beyond our barbed wire were parked two shiny limousines, each with a yellow flag flying from its bonnet and a soldier-chauffeur, duster at the ready, searching for any speck of dust that dared to land on the coachwork.

As we looked on, droning in towards the end of the runway came the reason for all the excitement and the abrupt interruption of our siesta. Two passenger planes touched down, bringing, so we were told later, a party of brasshats led by the Commander-in-Chief Java himself. Naturally we had to be there to greet him. We hoped that he appreciated that superbly-groomed runway. As the plane rolled to a halt, the limousines moved in, escorted by a fleet of assorted vehicles and ground troops. The tangled mass slowly resolved itself into a procession which began wending its way sedately towards us. At its heart each limousine was now closely followed by a lorry packed with troops, rifles and machine guns at the ready, no doubt to ensure that the brasshats continued to be treated with the appropriate fawning respect all along their route. We were kiosskied to attention until the long crocodile had passed out of sight. Then, the show over, we were allowed at long last to get back to our bamboos.

The next morning the whole circus returned and we were

marched out to join it and watch a demonstration of the striking power of the Nip fliers. It was nothing like so impressive as the bull of the Nip soldiers the previous evening. Dive-bomber after dive-bomber screamed down on those defenceless oil drums with singularly little effect. We felt that, if these were the men who were going to use our runway, our contribution to the Nip war effort wasn't going to unduly hamper the Allies after all.

The Nips did not let that contribution go entirely unrewarded. When the show ended we were marched back to a special lunch with a piece of bread, a chunk of cake and five fags per man. And for some of us the feasting did not stop there. The brasshats had lunched and watched the proceedings from a tent erected not far from our barbed wire. And, true to the form of pampered, overfed brasshats everywhere, they had ignored the food so painstakingly prepared for them. Standing against the wire we stared and stared at all that grub going to waste.

Then it happened. Perhaps it was the result of our combined will-power. More likely it was because the Nips were roaring drunk. Anyway a dozen of us were allowed to go scavenging at the brasshats' table. Looking back, no one with a grain of self respect would have taken up the offer. But we never gave it a second thought. We simply gloated over our good fortune and rushed to tuck in. Even then the celebrations were not yet over. Next afternoon the airfield commander, perhaps not yet sober, held his own little victory parade and took the salute from his 36 Nips, 300 Pows and a few assorted natives.

Keeping us all standing there, he let loose an impassioned address in Nipponese, of which, fortunately perhaps, 90 per cent of his audience couldn't understand a word. However he certainly kept the remaining ten per cent on their toes. Each time he referred to Dai Nippon his soldiers were obliged to spring smartly to attention. And as the sacred words cropped up about every other sentence even the most patriotic of the Nips began visibly to lose enthusiasm as the speech went on and on and on.

Between "Dai Nippons" we had the opportunity to scrutinise our Javanese fellow-workers, scarcely recognisable without their tattered shirts, threadbare shorts and bare feet. The Javanese too apparently had their fairy godmother, and she had transformed each one of them into an Eastern prince, with black fez, colourful batik sarong, shining white jacket and highly polished shoes.

Unfortunately their aura of wellbeing and prosperity wasn't to remain with them very long. For the commander now switched from Nip to Malay to deal with their wages. So far as we could understand, the Nipponese government, faced with soaring expenditure in its selfless struggle to build a glorious new world for the Asiatics, had been forced to bring in economies. In other words, pay was to be cut. But the Javanese should not grumble. They should appreciate the great sacrifices the Nipponese nation was making for them. In any case the workers were not to be left empty-handed. Each was to be presented immediately with a special scroll recording in Nipponese the service he had rendered to the Emperor.

It could be that at this point our Eastern princes found that their appreciation of their benefactors was fading. But they must have known all too well that even the most benevolent of Nips would not take too kindly to being told what to do with his scroll. They remained stonily silent.

So it was "On with the scrolls," and scrolls, even utterly worthless scrolls, are not something you simply push into the recipient's hand. They have to be given and received with due ceremony, especially if they happen to be Nip scrolls. Unfortunately, as you don't receive scrolls every day of the week, our princes were a little rusty on procedure. On hearing his name called, the lucky man had to approach within ten yards of the Nip handing out the wretched things, halt, bow deeply from the waist, and then advance and humbly wait for the correct moment in the little presentation speech for taking the scroll from the Nip's hand. He then had to retreat, walking backwards and keeping his eyes on the Nip, until he was clear of the ten-yard danger zone. Then, and only then, could he turn round and beat it. More than one of the favoured few had to be cuffed into the proper ritual, or had his scroll snatched from his grasp because he grabbed it too soon.

At length, all the scrolls disposed of, one way or another, the CO turned his attention to his coolies. He thanked us, on behalf of the glorious Nipponese army, for our long days of slaving in the sun. At one point it looked as though we might all be decorated with the Order of the Wilting Chrysanthemum, or some such. But instead the award was three quarters of a bottle of weak beer per man. It was a riotous night.

The morning after the night before was a sobering experience.

Instead of the promised yasmay day it was working parade as usual. The dive bombers had left three unexploded bombs somewhere in the swamp. The order was, 'Find them.' I had never felt that bomb disposal work was really me, so I spent the day paddling around knee-deep in ooze, making sure that I neither found nor disposed of anything. Fortunately suicidally-inclined comrades quickly unearthed two bombs, and long muddy hours later the third turned up. I kept my distance while the three were dragged together. They were then blown up... together with one over-enthusiastic Nip.

If we thought that our labours were over and that we could now lie back on our bamboos and dream of T-bone steaks, we were soon disillusioned. The very day after the bomb hunt we were back sweating on the runway. The Nips had overestimated the skill of their pilots. A wider area was needed for turning round the planes. But our slavemasters were no longer in such a fiendish hurry. We got time to wash our clothes, or what remained of them, and to organise a general clean-up. Perhaps the Nips had realised that we had begun to stink.

This interlude of comparative peace was marred by a tragedy in what we called the cookhouse, an atap roof supported by four bamboo poles. Our food was prepared in wejangs, huge conical cast-iron cooking pots, balanced on dwarf stone walls over log fires. We were waiting for the evening meal to be ladled out when the whisper went round that the mangy body of a kampong cat had been found floating in the stew wejang. We hoped that death was due to drowning after slipping off the roof, and not to rabies or some dread tropical disease. Nobody actually refused his meal, but the idea of even a healthy cat swimming in the stew did not improve our appetites. We had yet to rid outselves of our absurd fussiness over our food.

For once there seemed to be no rumours. And although deep down we knew they were all either grossly exaggerated or downright lies we got rather depressed without them. But fortunately there was generally local entertainment of some sort to give us a little psychological uplift. Like the day a crowded express on the main line alongside the airfield rolled to a halt leaving angry passengers stranded because the loco had run out of logs. Or when two trains met head-on on the same line and the drivers got out to harangue each other over who had the right of way.

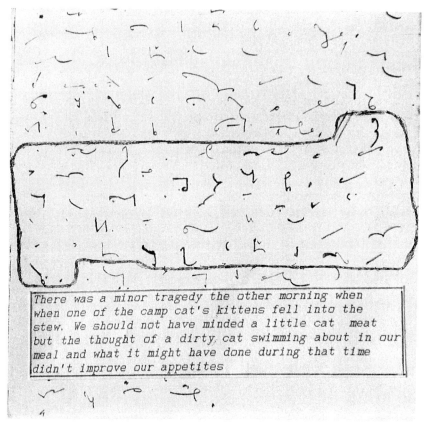

There was a minor tragedy the other morning when
when one of the camp cat's kittens fell into the
stew. We should not have minded a little cat meat
but the thought of a dirty cat swimming about in our
meal and what it might have done during that time
didn't improve our appetites

Diary extract from November 3, 1942

Then, as the airfield came into more constant use, we got a new morale-booster in the shape of the Nip air force. A bomber pilot, who dropped in unexpectedly, delighted us with a skidding broadside that would have done credit to a dirt-track ace when he noticed, rather belatedly, that our light railway lay right across his path. It was several days before his plane was fit to take off again. There was a slapstick serial provided by a gang trying to get a plane into the air pulling a drogue target. Time after time the target caught on some obstruction or other, the rope snapped, the whiplash scattered the Nips, and the plane took off towing nothing but a piece of string.

Dive-bombing practice was often great fun too, with the bombs tending to fall anywhere but on the target. One pilot made a very creditable attempt to close the main railway line. But we were not always in the best position to appreciate the joke. We had one or two narrow escapes.

Towards the end of November the rains came in earnest. Some days the torrential downpour completely walled us off from the rest of the world. Our wretched huts stood alone in a watery waste. Rain poured through the leaky atap on to our bedding. We huddled in groups, cold and utterly miserable. Worse, the Nips began to see the advantage of having drains, and had us up to our knees in mud digging them. For many the gluey going meant the end of what remained of their footwear. We went out to work barefoot, but fortunately the soles of our feet seemed to have hardened as our footwear deteriorated and we managed better than expected.

A new Nip sergeant took charge of the rations. He was quite mad, due, it was said, to syphilis. It was simply asking for injury to go anywhere near him. But oddly enough our food improved, and with the bad weather we had never felt more in need of a square meal. Despite everything some found the lack of a smoke was a real hardship. Changes in our work pattern had cut off the trickle of local tobacco we had been getting from the natives. Addicts were reduced to hunting for fag ends dropped by the Nips. Some of the more enterprising managed to wheedle complete cigarettes out of the less hostile Nips. One prisoner claimed to have amassed twenty in twos and threes by proffering the same ten cent note to different guards and asking if he could buy a couple.

Then the constant hunger, the incessant rain, the stinking work and the tobacco famine became more bearable as we were swept up in yet another whirlwind of general euphoria. This time we were going to be out for Christmas, now little more than a month away. Hopes for this miracle were based on a promise alleged to have been made to all Allied prisoners by no less a person than President Roosevelt. Anyone who faced the facts knew it was lunacy, but it was lunacy to face the facts. Our optimism was also fed by the huge formations of Nip bombers and fighters we saw day after day passing overhead heading east. Could it be that the Allied invasion of Timor, still well up in the top ten rumours, was true and the Nips were having to throw in everything they'd got to counter it?

Almost ignored at our news conference in the drain we were digging at the time was a claim that the Americans had landed in North Africa. And, oddly enough, I discovered years later, they had. The Nips gave us December 8 off to celebrate Pearl Harbour. We prayed that the Americans were giving them something suitable to mark the occasion. Time soon caught up with the 'Out by Christmas' dream, but like the 'Help from the Hills' sermon and the Rice Legend, it had served its purpose. It had kept our spirits up for a while. And anyway there would be plenty of other Christmasses to be out by. But Christmas 1942 was with us. Christmas was a time to make merry, and we decided to do just that.

Three ramshackle huts in a ring of barbed wire on the edge of a Javanese swamp didn't seem a particularly appropriate setting for the holly and mistletoe festivities. But we had a day off. And already an off-white balloon was floating over one hut door. Someone had finally decided that the contraceptive he had been holding on to for the past year was not really likely to fulfil its destined rôle.

Whatever the big occasion, be it a Coronation, a penny off a pint of beer, or the sinking of the *Titanic,* the reflex action of the Army and the Air Force seems to be to organise a football match. So it was something in the nature of a Christmas treat not to have one. But, weary as we were from our labours on the runway, it would have been too much to expect completely to escape the traditional imposition of some sporting activity. In the end it was decided that we should mark our first Christmas as coolies with a game of cricket.

Jimmy, Bert and I had far better things to do, like stretching out on our bamboos planning in detail our Christmas cook-up. We were just discussing how to get the utmost satisfaction out of the egg, onions and fruit we had managed to acquire when Jimmy revealed his big secret. Rummaging in the depths of his tattered kitbag he produced, to our absolute amazement, a tin of genuine British bully beef. How he had managed for nine whole months, while we were all obsessed with food, not only to resist the temptation to eat it, but also to avoid giving even the slightest hint of its existence, is beyond my comprehension. He couldn't have given us a bigger surprise had he produced an oven-ready turkey. With Jimmy's fantastic contribution, our purchases, and the rice ration from the cookhouse, we produced what seemed at the time a truly magnificent spread. Full stomachs, sweet coffee and Java cheroots produced a marvellous feeling of wellbeing. I'd never appreciated a Christmas dinner more. At the evening tenko the Nips weighed in with their present. We were each given a postcard to send home: a chance to let our families know we were still alive.

We didn't even have to worry about what to write. The Nips had decided for us. They gave us a list of twelve sentences from which we were allowed to choose three. No. 1 read "We prisoners of war are allowed to write to you by courtesy of the generous Japanese Government." Others, in similar vein, said we were being well treated, we were well or not well, and so forth. All that was missing was "Wish you were here" to sign off with. We filled in the cards eagerly, in the hope of getting at least some sort of message home. Of course we didn't realise that few of these cards or any that we wrote later would ever reach their destination.

In our Christmas stockings we each received a piece of soap, some toothpaste and a little towel. Where they came from we never knew. Certainly the "generous Japanese Government" would never have dreamed of supplying prisoners with such luxuries. It can only have been yet another act of kindness from those indomitable Ladies of Semarang, though how they got the local Nip commander to play Santa I can't imagine. According to the camp grapevine they had also sent in 300 food parcels which were even then stocked in the Nip quarters. But if the parcels ever existed they certainly never reached us.

The Nips' big festival was on New Year's Day, which we were told was every Nip's official birthday. A photographer arrived at their quarters presumably to record the high jinks for their folks back home. But as we watched through the barbed wire we could see that the communal birthday cake was a lump of concrete with a sprinkling of flour on top and the bottles of beer were empties filled with water. They did have real children to pose with them. They had been imported from the nearby kampong. But they were quickly shooed away once the photographer had got his phoney pictures.

On January 4 the hundred Dutch who had shared our fortunes for the last six months suddenly left us. We presumed they were being taken back to Surabaya.

Then the rains, which had mercifully eased off over Christmas resumed with increased fury. The camp became one with the swamp. Even the Nips agreed that work was impossible. Everything in the huts turned wet and clammy.

Though we were within a few degrees of the Equator it was impossible to keep warm. We shivered under our tattered blankets, discussed the latest absurd rumours and talked about food.

Soon the first cases of dysentery and beri-beri, two diseases that were to be our constant companions for the rest of our imprisonment, began to appear. Malaria continued unabated. I was recovering, painfully slowly this time, from my eighth attack, one for every month in Semarang. It was dysentery that had the most devastating effect on the camp. By the end of the month 22 men had been carried off to hospital in Semarang, eight more were in isolation in camp, and some 60 more were ill. The Nips had us all inoculated, and shot three stray kampong dogs just to be on the safe side, but the epidemic continued unabated. Another five men were sent off to hospital, but they were back by return of post, together with all the other hospital cases, irrespective of their condition. We were on the move again.

This time the Nips took no chances of a triumphal march through Semarang with women showering us with cakes and cigarettes. At dusk on February 5 we were shepherded into a train waiting in the sand wagon sidings on the airfield.

We had settled down for the night as best we could on our wooden benches when at 11.40 an engine clanked into our coaches and we were on our way. We didn't get very far, no farther in fact than Semarang station. There we were shunted into another siding for the rest of the night.

At 9.30 next morning our coaches were attached to a passenger–cum–goods train. Still recovering from my malaria, I travelled in what could loosely be called the hospital coach. Many men were very ill. For them it was a terrible journey. We stopped at every station. It was often all we could do to keep the sick on their stretchers as we were jolted about by the clumsy, noisy shunting on, or dropping off, of coaches and trucks.

As darkness was falling we were still rattling along. Once more through the windows of brightly-lit bungalows alongside the track we had tantalising glimpses of the sort of domestic scenes which for us were no more than a fading memory. A family gathered round a dining table, a wife ironing a few clothes, a grandfather dozing in an armchair.

Finally at about 9 p.m., more than 24 hours after boarding the train, we pulled into Surabaya station.

6: BEWARE OF THE BULL

February - April, 1943. Jaarmarkt Camp, Surabaya, Java

It was too dark to see much of the Jaarmarkt camp when we arrived, but we scarcely noticed. We were too busy sniffing. On the night breeze, as we were counted, recounted and counted again, came a heavenly aroma. And wonderful as it was, it still didn't do justice to its source. For when the Nips had finally decided that they hadn't mislaid anyone en route, we were marched off to sample the sort of stew we'd forgotten existed.

As soon as we had hungrily wolfed it down we were hustled in the gloom across a large parade ground to some bamboo-framed atap huts. I found myself in a shack perhaps about 100 ft long. The top half of each side was open but was provided with atap shutters. A bamboo sleeping platform ran along either side with a gangway down the middle. There were doorless doorways at either end. This was my new home.

Before we had even had time to unpack our kit, old friends we had last seen at Tasikmalaya came tumbling in to swap experiences. But almost immediately a bugle sounded lights out. And with a quick warning to "Beware of the Bull" our pals scattered. It was a camp rule that everyone must be in his billet by lights out, and at Jaarmarkt, as we discovered next day, rules were not to be flouted. The place was run by a vicious bunch of Korean guards who made the Nips seem quite reasonable. The Bull turned out to be a particularly brutish sample whose hobby was patrolling the huts looking for someone to beat up.

'Jaarmarkt' means a fairground, and some remnants of the old structures remained. Some of the Dutch prisoners were housed incongruously in what appeared to have been an oriental tunnel of love. The whole area was surrounded by a high bamboo wall broken at intervals by sentry towers manned at all times by armed guards. It was by far the biggest of the fourteen camps I was in during my three and a half years with the Nips. I can't say how many of us were incarcerated there but there were certainly a few thousand. The British were nearly all RAF with a sprinkling of Army and Navy lads.

The sailors were survivors from the destroyer *Jupiter*, one of four British warships lost in the Battle of the Java Sea. The *Jupiter* lads had learned their new rôle in life very quickly. After sinking, they told us, they had struggled to the safety of dry land only to be met by a Nip invasion force. It seemed that at that time nothing could go wrong for the Nips. Just when they needed coolies, a bunch of half-drowned Brits came crawling up the beach.

The majority of the Jaarmarkt inmates were Dutch. Some had been well-heeled Surabaya businessmen until the invasion wrecked their lives. They either had large sums of money with them, or access to it on the outside. They had got themselves, and somewhere along the line some Nips or Koreans too, very well-organised. And they were generous enough to spread the benefits around. As a result Jaarmarkt had by far the best food I came

The brave little HMS Jupiter, *one of the tiny force of Allied warships which sailed gallantly out to take on the might of the Nip navy in the Battle of the Java Sea. The author met survivors in the Jaarmarkt prison camp. (Imperial War Museum)*

across as a Pow. Incredibly there were even occasional handouts of eggs, bananas and sugar, all acquired somehow by the Dutch. We half-naked newcomers were also treated to a handout of badly-needed clothing. I was fortunate enough to acquire an old green Dutch Army tunic and a more or less matching pair of shorts.

But everything in life has to be paid for, particularly in Pow life. And the price of the Jaarmarkt goodies was the Jaarmarkt discipline. It began with the dawn bugle call. We were hounded out of our huts on to the camp square, hounded by a bunch of whooping Koreans competing with each other for the pleasure of beating up any stragglers. On the square, encouraged by more Koreans yelling "Koorah" at frequent intervals, we formed ourselves into what could loosely be called a parade, facing east. Then, as the light of the bright new day tinged the sentry towers with rose, a falsetto Korean voice shrieked "Ki-oss-ki", and those on the fringes of the parade brought themselves grudgingly to something like attention. "Kirri," screamed the voice, and those under the close scrutiny of the surrounding guards bowed stiffly to the rising sun and its close relative the Emperor Hirohito.

Prisoners fortunate enough to be in the middle of the parade and hidden from the Koreans, followed a different ritual. They spat on the ground and intoned what could be roughly translated as "To hell with Hirohito," but in rather stronger language.

Then there were the interminable tenkos. Our hosts seemed haunted by the fear that somehow, somewhere, someone was missing. They lined us up two deep. Counted us from the front, counted us from the rear. Counted heads, counted feet. They then worked out little sums in the dust with sticks, and started out all over again. Even this farcical procedure did not completely reassure them, so they forced us to number in Nipponese. As every mistake meant a clout across the face, most of us could soon number as quickly in Nipponese as in English. One or two lads simply could not remember the Nip numbers, so we kept them in the back row. The Koreans got wise to this and kept turning parades back to front to give themselves a few extra faces to slap.

The star turn of this pantomime was a flight lieutenant who, after a particularly rough numbering session, was ordered to punish the parade. Quick as a flash, arms waving, he launched into what must be the most ferocious rendering ever of "Mary Had a Little Lamb." The guards beamed contentedly as we strove to keep straight faces.

Naturally we reverted to the bowing and saluting regime we had endured at the Lyceum. Hair that had grown to a respectable length in lax Semarang had to be cut to the roots. We also had to follow a precise routine on feeling the call of nature after curfew. The procedure was to approach the nearest sentry tower, wait until you were sure you had been observed, bow and then bawl out: "Banjo Mickey Mouse!" This unlikely combination apparently bears some resemblance to "May I go to the toilet?" in Nipponese.

The "toilet" turned out to be a super-luxury latrine by Pow standards. No open-trench fly metropolis here. Instead, sunk into the ground, we found a huge metal tank with holes spaced out over the surface at appropriate distances. To watch the once high and mighty Europeans at this mass squat must have given great satisfaction to our guards, but at least it was all very hygienic. It appeared, however, that this bizarre multi-loo could have been installed for economic rather than health reasons, for quite incredibly the Nips made money out of it. A contractor came along from time to time to drain out the tank with a suction pump, and paid quite handsomely for the privilege. For while the Nips may have demoted the white man from demi-god to coolie, the manure he produced was still at a premium to the Asiatic variety.

On March 8, from over the bamboo wall, came the joyous sounds of music, singing and dancing punctuated by fireworks. The Javanese were celebrating the anniversary of their 'liberation' by the Nips.

On our side of the wall we quietly took stock of our first year in the bag. Accepting that beatings and face slapping were an integral part of the Nip soldier's way of life, those of us from Semarang could not complain that we had been subjected to much brutality. But there were ominous warnings from prisoners who had been in other camps.

At Malang a sergeant and warrant officer had made the only serious attempt at escaping that I had heard of so far. The WO, a Eurasian, possessed a sound knowledge of the island and its languages and they reckoned on being able to make their way to the coast and find a boat. Instead the Javanese police found them, and handed them over to the Nips, who promptly shot them. Not quite Geneva Convention, but not unexpected.

Then there was the case of a flight lieutenant and a pilot officer who, bored with life at Malang, wandered through the camp gates bent on a night out in the local kampong. They too were picked up by the busy Javanese police and taken back to camp. The Nip commandant, realising that they hadn't the slightest intention of escaping, ordered a series of daily beatings. But, as these were being carried out, he received orders from the top brass. They must be shot. Both the commandant and the camp guards, it appeared, were genuinely sorry, but Nips didn't dispute orders. The whole camp was assembled to watch from a distance as the sentence was carried out. This was sheer bloody murder.

At the Lyceum camp, some time after we had left it for Semarang, two Ambonese had gone over the wall to see their families. They, too had been caught by the industrious Javanese police. Back in the camp they were tied up against a couple of palm trees and beaten savagely at each changing of the guard, day and night. This went on for a fortnight, after which the two now half-crazed men were moved into a cage of wooden stakes and barbed wire. Here not only did the beatings continue, but refinements were added. The men stood on sharpened pieces of bamboo, suffering thrashings every time they fell off. Guards poked stakes into their ears and mouths. Often the whole camp was kept awake, fearful and helpless, as their cries echoed on throughout the night. They were still in their cage when the camp was evacuated and the rest of the prisoners moved to the Jaarmarkt.

We wondered just what kind of men our captors could be to commit such an atrocity, and shuddered to think that our lives were in their hands. Even after these reports I don't think many of us realised just how precarious our lives had become. In fact the arrival in camp of an ornate hearse drawn by four black-plumed, black-coated horses for the burial of one of the wealthier Dutch came as something as a shock. It still hadn't dawned that a great many of us would never get back home.

Meanwhile, for the moment, life could have been a lot worse. True the guards continued their campaign to make the days as miserable as possible, but our anti-Korean alarm system managed to foil them most of the time.

Jaarmarkt was a world in miniature. There were the idle rich among the Dutch who somehow contrived to be able to sit playing chess and drinking coffee all day. There were the wheeler-dealers buying and selling a remarkable range of goods. There were conmen and cardsharpers. And, of course, there were the

68

long-suffering underdogs, who included practically all the poverty-stricken British.

Seeing how the other half lived did not increase our enthusiasm for outside working-parties. Rolling barrels of petrol, heaving bombs about, or digging drains, all for ten cents a day, was a mug's game. So I considered myself lucky when our MO declared me unfit for further outside work.

This qualified me for a job in the camp rope factory. Here we earned our ten cents sitting in rows on the floor, twiddling a spindle with our toes and plaiting strands of sisal fibre into a thick coarse string with our fingers. As we also got some back pay from Semarang, Jim, Bert and I were able to indulge ourselves with a little private cooking. We bought from the Dutch various sorts of tropical beans and something resembling horse-radish which, together with leaves found growing around the camp, made what we were sure was a vitamin-rich soup.

Jaarmarkt's air of permanency raised fond hopes that we might be there for the duration, so we started planning for the future. First we appropriated a little plot to grow weeds to provide leaves for soups. Then we looked to our finances. Surveying the activities of the old hands among the Dutch we decided we could do much worse than get into the ting-ting business. This required some expensive capital equipment, so we pooled our resources. At great expense we acquired one battered tin helmet which had somehow escaped confiscation and been converted into a frying pan. A little more outlay, on groundnuts and palm sugar, and we were on our way. We roasted the nuts, mixed them with melted sugar, then poured the gooey result on to a flat surface. When it cooled it produced a brittle toffee. This was ting-ting which, provided you hadn't burnt the sugar, sold at twice the cost of the raw materials. We soon recouped our investment and told ourselves we were headed for the big time. If only it could have lasted.

However, before the next blow fell, we went to the pictures. Or, perhaps more accurately, the pictures came to us. We were called out on parade and ordered to squat down in lines in front of a large screen which had been erected on the camp square. The film we were shown must be the original war-in-the-Pacific epic, grandfather of all those American blood-and-thunders which have been rivalling even the Westerns on TV screens ever since. Of course it didn't show the Yanks as the conquering heroes. That rôle, naturally, was filled by the Nips. It covered their fantastic run of successes before John Wayne took a hand to redress the balance, showing the attack on Pearl Harbour, the sinking of the *Prince of Wales* and the *Repulse* and the death-throes of a British aircraft carrier off Ceylon. And no Hollywood mock-ups these. They appeared to be the real thing filmed during the attacks. There was no attempt to whitewash the treachery of Pearl Harbour. The film gloried in the fact that the Americans were taken completely by surprise. One sequence portrayed a Hawaii radio announcer pleading with his listeners to believe that what he was telling them was no radio drama, no military exercise but real bloody war.

We watched in silence. What surprised us most was that the Nips should want to show us it at all. We were surely the last people who needed propaganda to convince us that the Nips were winning. And who cared a rap what Pows thought anyway? Perhaps in a crazy sort of way that only the Nips could be expected to understand it was a sort of recruitment exercise. Because only a few days later 2000 of us were told we were being drafted to work with the Nip army. The little world of Jaarmarkt had been too good to last.

Of course the Nips didn't take just anyone in their labour battalion. Everyone had to have a medical examination. So we were hauled out on parade. Then what we assumed was a Nip MO, seated smoking at a little table on the camp square, gave each man a thorough stare at a range of 20 feet or so as we were herded briskly past him. Although I had only recently been adjudged unfit for Jaarmarkt's normal outside working-parties I was not really surprised to find myself chosen for this élite task force. But it distressed me when Bert, still having serious eye troubles and not really fit to walk round the block, also passed the stringent test. Jim, who had just gone down with dysentery, didn't even make the starting post, so I was separated from the last member of my old unit, No 1 MTRS.

The chosen were called out for a special parade next day, notable for the extra bawling and extra kow-towing among the extra numbers of less than normally scruffy guards. All this heralded the arrival of a Nip major, a big man by Nip standards, with a wispy goat beard and an evil grin, a sort of latter day Kublai Khan. Nitty Whiskers, as he quickly became known, gave a speech in tolerable English. We would be sent away, he said, to work with the Nip-

Nitty Whiskers, drawn by an unknown artist. 'The Nipponese army will protect you', he told prisoners before they sailed to build airstrips in the islands. He didn't say who would protect them from the Nip army

ponese army. We would be well treated and well fed. The Nipponese army would protect us. If we worked hard we had nothing to worry about. We started worrying there and then. Where were were going that we would need the protection of the Nip army? What did the Nips mean by "well fed and well treated?" What would happen if we didn't, or couldn't, work "hard" in their estimation?

Next came the issue of kit for the mission: one pair of tree-climbing, separate-toe, rubber boots per man, the only clothing issue I received from the Nips in three and a half years.

One Dutchman in the party, well shod but perhaps not-so-well equipped upstairs, thought he would save the generous Nip army even the pair of boots. He took the liberty of indicating that he didn't need nor want them. Not many fitted the recipients anyway. The guards seemed to take this as a gross insult to the Emperor himself and gave the unfortunate prisoner so savage a beating up that he had to be carted off to hospital.

As a sort of condemned man's breakfast we were each allowed to send a second card home, or at any rate we thought it was going home. Then at dawn on April 18, after a night worrying where our mystery tour would take us, and wearing my new tree-climbing boots, I marched out of Jaarmarkt.

7: THE GOOD SHIP CHO SAKI MARU

April-May, 1943. At Sea, Java to South Moluccas

Hopes that we might yet avoid a cruise with Nippon Tours rose when our march from Jaarmarkt took us no further than the local railway station. After all, reasoned the optimists, the Nips would hardly provide a train to take a couple of thousand miserable prisoners the five or six miles to the sea. But once again the Nips showed their unpredictability and, after an hour of being shunted from siding to siding, we ended up where we least wanted to be: Tanjong Perak docks.

There we were sprayed from head to foot by Nips carrying on their backs tanks of what was presumably some sort of disinfectant. Whether this was for our benefit or to stop us contaminating the ships was not clear. Then we were quickly herded on to lighters. And as we left the docks we noticed, with some consternation, that we were heading for some small grey cargo boats anchored a little way out. As our lighter passed under the bows of a forbidding-looking ship of perhaps 8000 tons, I caught a glimpse of her name, *Cho Saki Maru*. Bert and I were among 1000 prisoners driven aboard her.

Three holds had been fitted with shelves to carry extra bodies. Our hold seemed already grossly overcrowded when Bert and I were shoved down. But still more and more men were pushed in behind us. Eventually there were 410 of us crammed into an area some 40 to 50 feet square. At first it looked as though many of us would have to spend the voyage standing up, but after a while we managed to organise ourselves so that everyone had his little bit of floor space.

In the hold, just above our heads there was an ironic reminder of home. Stamped on a girder were the words "Made in Skinningrove, England." Somewhere no more than 30 miles from my birthplace. For, despite her name, the *Cho Saki Maru* was an old British ship, no doubt one of the many sold to the Nips before the war as "scrap."

It was a hot day, even by Javanese standards, and with the sun beating down through the open hatches the stench of sweaty bodies quickly became overpowering. One way of getting a little respite from this hell-hole was to take a trip to the latrines: two orange-box contraptions hung over the ship's rail. Here we could squat out over the waves in glorious sunshine cooled by the sea breezes. Of course we all wanted to go at once. Of course the armed Nip guarding our hatchway became more than a little truculent. But at length a compromise was reached. Small batches of men were allowed up on deck in turn to take in their oxygen ration.

After the long hot day in the hold, dusk came as a welcome relief. But after a couple of hours a tropical storm broke over us. The hatches had to be covered to stop us drowning. So it was a long sweaty night.

Next morning we waited impatiently in considerable discomfort for the hatch covers to be removed. Dawn light silhouetted the guard at the hatchway, the ship rocked gently at her anchor, but all remained quiet overhead. It seemed hours later that the covers were at long last lifted off and, to our intense relief, an awning was erected to shield our sweatpit from the scorching sun. Breakfast arrived: a miserly helping of rice pap with the inevitable fat weevil grubs embalmed in it.

Then, as we were just settling down to a day of hot, sticky boredom, a tremendous explosion rocked the ship. Those on deck taking their air ration were quickly hustled back below. We lay there in an untidy heap apprehensively eyeing the one set of iron rungs that led out of the hold, and the armed Nip at the top of them. We hadn't a clue as to what was going on. There had been no sound of planes or gunfire. We were sure of only one thing: that if the ship sank we would sink too, like rats in the proverbial trap.

Tense minutes dragged by. Nothing seemed to be happening. Gradually tension began to ease. After a while a few men were allowed back on deck again. They found the ship unscathed. Everything was as it had been except that our apprehension about our cruise was greater than ever. And our fears weren't lessened by the story of the blast which eventually trickled down to us through the usual unspecified, totally unreliable sources. A ship anchored beside us, the story ran, had caught fire and blown up, killing 100 Javanese and 60 Pows as they tried to get off.

However when our second and final meal of the day arrived we decided we were more likely to die of starvation than any act of violence. It consisted of a small mugful of steamed rice and a few spoonfuls of watery stew. This, together with the morning pap, was to be our daily ration for the whole of the trip. We spent the next day waiting impatiently for our turns on the deck and hungrily for our two meals.

It was 1 p.m. on our fourth day on the boat when we heard the anchor rattling up. Those on deck were hurriedly pushed back down the hold. The vibration of the engines shook our little inferno and we were on our way to God knew where.

Lying below decks with not even a pocket compass and unable to see the sun, even a Drake might have found it difficult to chart our course. But we had our barrack-room navigators. They had us sailing north up the strait dividing Java from Madura, the smaller island which fits into the step nature cut out of the mainland's north-east corner. That evening, after sightings taken from the latrine boxes, we were said to be sailing west along the north coast of Java, in convoy with four other cargo ships, a small motor vessel and an escort of two destroyers. Sumatra became a firm favourite in the destination betting-stakes.

However, when we were allowed back on deck next day, which someone somehow discovered was Good Friday, the convoy was chugging in calm seas towards the east with land to starboard. Our navigators explained that we had turned completely round during the night, retraced our course, and were now off the north coast of Madura. Two miserable meals later, with the sun sinking behind us, land petered out, and, after passing three last small islands, we headed into an empty sea, so far as most of us were concerned completely lost.

Next morning all became brilliantly clear. Away to starboard, floodlit by the rising sun, were the magnificent mountains of Bali rising in gaunt grandeur up to the sacred Gunung Agung itself. Bali, the fabulous paradise island, steeped in Hindu culture, famed for its temples and topless dancing girls, and now overrun by Nips. We wondered what they would all be having for breakfast. By evening we were off the less spectacular, but nevertheless splendidly rugged, island of Lombok. Viewed from our sea-view latrine, with the rusting old ship and the Nips well out of sight

The prisoner's fantasy. We sat on our orange box loos strung over the side of the Cho Saki Maru, *stared longingly at the rugged outline of Bali, and dreamt our dreams*

behind us, the tang of the sea in our nostrils and a fantastic sunset setting the gently heaving waves aflame, Lombok provided the sort of scene millionaires might have paid a fortune to enjoy. We would have preferred to see a plate of fish and chips.

Easter Sunday found our convoy sailing through clusters of desolate-looking islets, many of them mere hunks of rock rising sheer from the ocean. Even the larger ones bore no vegetation other than a few stunted bushes growing in the watercourses.

In the absence of a swimming pool the Nips rigged up a pump so that we could hose ourselves down with seawater. We were all now able to spend long spells on deck. But the food situation did not improve. Our rations were worse than they had ever been on land, and now there was no chance of buying, borrowing or stealing that little extra that meant so much. Two of the cargo ships left the convoy, taking a more southerly course. Our amateur navigators reckoned they must be going to Timor, that island of shark-infested-sea fame which only a few weeks previously General Rumour had retaken for the Allies.

Suddenly, as a reminder that there was still a war going on somewhere, the Nips sounded battle stations. We were pushed roughly into our hold. The ship appeared to turn full circle. We again sat nervously surveying that one set of iron rungs and speculating just what had caused the alert. But there was no sign of a plane, submarine or warship, or whatever it was the Nips feared, and we soon returned to the deck.

On Monday we sailed through a group of small misty islands, some no more than the tops of half-submerged volcanoes. There was another alarm. Again we were herded back into the hold. Again that anxious wait. But our luck held out.

Then on the Wednesday morning we found the ship heading straight for land: a lush dark green island, contrasting sharply with any we had seen since leaving Java. Soon we were sailing up a narrow channel between thickly-wooded hills with native houses and wooden huts here and there among the trees. We nosed alongside a small pier backed by corrugated iron buildings which seemed to house some sort of army unit. Word came down on the grapevine that we had arrived in Ambon, one of the southernmost islands of the Moluccas, the spice islands of the history books.

Ambon had been a big naval base of the Dutch until the Nips had relieved them of it, but we had apparently sneaked in by the back door for there was nothing to be seen apart from the little jetty. The Nips started unloading cargo almost before the boat had stopped, but we were not disturbed and it soon became evident that this was not the end of our voyage.

Next day, April 29, seemed just another routinely boring sort of day when we were allowed on deck and found the ship still at the jetty. But suddenly we were startled by the staccato pumping of

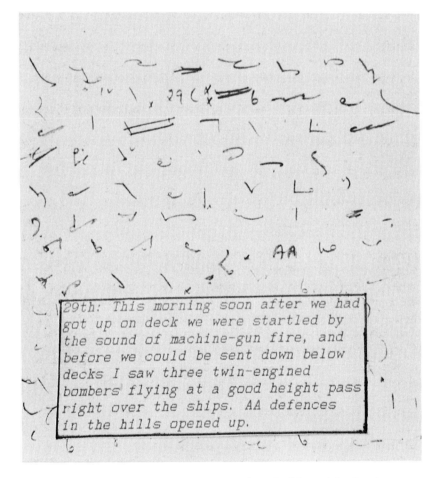

29th: This morning soon after we had got up on deck we were startled by the sound of machine-gun fire, and before we could be sent down below decks I saw three twin-engined bombers flying at a good height pass right over the ships. AA defences in the hills opened up.

Diary extract from April 29, 1943. Emperor Hirohito's birthday and the Americans were trying to make it a day to remember. Our first real evidence since becoming prisoners that the war was still on

78

machine-gun fire from somewhere close by. And straight over-head, at no more than two or three thousand feet, came three American twin-engined bombers. Anti-aircraft guns opened up in the hills around us.

At this point I was forced back down into the hold, but those who managed to stay on deck just a little longer saw more bombers coming along behind. It was, we discovered, the Emperor's birthday and the Allies were calling with an appropriate present.

After thirteen months as prisoners we were excited at this first sign that someone was fighting back, though we hoped they'd watch just who they were dropping their bombs on. Despite the raid, or perhaps because of it, the ship stayed at the jetty all day. And when we moved off next morning it was only to anchor in the channel close to the open sea.

Opposite our anchorage, at the foot of those green hills and half-hidden among coconut palms, we saw the atap roofs of a little kampong, whose fishing boats were drawn up on the dazzlingly white beach in front of it. Just another glimpse of a mini-paradise so near and yet so far away.

We moved off at dusk, and next morning, Saturday May 1, we came up on deck to find the ship at anchor in a landlocked bay close in to a landing stage around which clustered a few atap huts. A few hours later the Nips ordered a small party of us into sampans and we were ferried ashore. I don't suppose that we had been singled out for an afternoon's relaxation, but some Nip some-where had blundered. No one ashore was looking for coolies and we were left lazing in the delicious shade of a huge tree. Before being ordered back on board a couple of hours later we learned that we had arrived at Amahai, a small town on the island of Ceram, next door to New Guinea.

Work started in earnest at midnight the next day, unloading our ship. It was then that we discovered that there really had not been much need to worry about going down with her. We were much more likely to have been blown sky high or incinerated. We had been sleeping on a cargo of 250 lb bombs and barrels of petrol stacked in the hold immediately beneath us.

However that was now history. The immediate problem was how best to manhandle the bloody things. They were ferried by sampan to dropping points along the shore, and then it was our job to lug them through the semi-jungle to inland dumps. The barrels we could roll and then upend and cartwheel over obstacles, but moving the bombs was purgatory. With the usual encouragement from the Nips we nevertheless eventually found a way. After the bombs and the petrol the unloading of the *Cho Saki Maru* became one gigantic lucky dip. Again and again her derricks swung round to delve among a higgledy-piggledy assortment of edible roots, beans, picks and shovels, wheat, rice and the odd steamroller, all packed in thousands and thousands of loose oranges.

Then came the last of her cargo, the thousand prisoners. We were crammed on to the deck of a tiny coaster. Our journey was not quite yet over. Four hours later nightfall found us chugging through a weirdly green, glassy sea towards a black silhouette which was to be our home for the next eighteen months. Our guards had no more idea of where we were than we had, but eventually a Nip sailor came up with the name "Uruck."

And so, late on the night of May 4, sixteen days after boarding the *Cho Saki Maru*, we reached the tiny island of Haruku, the last home for many, and for those who came back a name which will forever remain synonymous with disease, despair and death.

8: THE BAMBOO GUNZO

May, 1943. Haruku, South Moluccas

We were ferried ashore in native canoes at midnight, and in pitch blackness we stumbled on to a stony beach. From there, guided by the odd flickering candle stuck in the trunk of a coconut palm, we forced our way through dripping undergrowth, cursing as we tripped over tree roots, or slipped in the slime and collapsed in a heap with our belongings on top of us. At length, bruised and scratched by thorns, we reached some half-built atap huts. Utterly exhausted, we sank down in the mud inside and fell asleep.

We woke, hungry and muddy, to a damp cheerless dawn. The huts, we found, were in an overgrown grove of dripping coconut palms and nutmeg trees. But coconuts on the tree are useless unless you happen to be a particularly agile monkey, and to a hungry man the nutmeg is just about the most idiotic fruit nature has ever produced.

One side of the camp was bounded by the sea. From it a tall barbed wire fence swung out past the huts to enclose a swamp, and then ran down into a valley to enclose a short stretch of a stream before turning back to the shore. By the stream stood our cookhouse, which that morning was unable to produce anything to eat or even drink.

But we had little time to dwell on our misery. Supplies had to be ferried ashore from our ships: more bombs, more barrels of petrol to be dragged up the beach in the rain. Late that night we staggered wearily back to the huts. Native carpenters had finished off the roofs during the day but, even more important, the cook-house had produced its first food. We slithered down into the valley, barking our shins on tree stumps in the dark, eager to get a mess-tin of pap. Then it was back up again to doss down in the mud.

After an all-night struggle to keep the fires burning in the rain, the cookhouse managed to have another mess-tin of pap all round ready for us at dawn. But we had scarcely time to swallow it down before a squad of bellowing Nips came rampaging through the huts to herd us into a clearing intended for the camp square. They lined us up in twos, counted and recounted. There were 2075 of us: 1000 from the *Cho Saki Maru* and the rest from one of the other ships in the convoy from Surabaya. Stocktaking over, half of us, including Bert and me, were marched through the barbed wire fence by a party of Nip soldiers. A narrow track between tall trees led us to a kampong of atap houses. Our guards escorted us through a throng of wildly-excited islanders and out into the tree-less hills beyond the village. We finally halted between two huge overgrown humps of coral which seemed to form the backbone of the island.

Here we learned the purpose of Operation Haruku. The Nips wanted the tops of these two humps sliced off and deposited in the intervening valley to provide an airstrip. And we prisoners with our usual chunkels, Chinese wheelbarrows and cut-down shopping baskets, supplemented by a few tiny toffee hammers and some giant chisels, were going to do it.

Setting ourselves the target of looking busy enough to keep the Nips happy while expending the minimum of effort, we set about this seemingly impossible task. By this time many of us were in the early stages of dysentery and the large numbers of men constantly downing tools to go into the surrounding bush for a banjo soon exhausted the Nips' very limited patience. Kicks in the guts and clouts across the back with rifle butts became frequent. Shortly after midday the other half of coolie battalion arrived on the coral. We handed over our hammers, chisels, chunkels and Chinese wheelbarrows and marched thankfully back to camp and a mess-tin of pap.

The skies had cleared and it was now hot and sunny. Just the afternoon to spend some time blissfully wallowing in the cool, clear waters of the stream as we enjoyed our first fresh-water wash for three weeks. We then washed our stinking clothes native-style, bashing them on rocks in the stream, and hung them on bushes to dry.

Our half-day shift set the pattern for work in the early days on the airstrip. Slowly the cookhouse got itself organised and began to produce three meals a day, though they were pitifully inadequate: pap for breakfast and midday, and steamed rice with a few spoonfuls of watery stew at night. For the first four days on the island the cookhouse failed to produce anything at all to drink. We relied on rainwater which we caught in our mess-tins as it poured off the hut roofs. Frequent storms drenched us at work during the day and left us wet and cold at night. Gradually the local carpenters installed shelves along the sides of the huts. At least we could now sleep clear of the mud. This just about raised our living conditions to the intolerable.

Nominally in charge of our welfare, as camp commandant, was a slight bespectacled Nip officer said to have been a stationmaster before being called up. But the real boss was a bull-like sergeant whose square head seemed to be stuck directly on to his massive slightly rounded shoulders. Little of his face could be seen as he always wore his peaked hat pulled well down over his forehead and he was rarely seen without his dark sunglasses.

Gunzo Mori, the Bamboo Gunzo, beat dysentery patients with his bamboo pole and sent them off to work. But he had a sympathetic grunt for Peacock, allowed back to his hut because he was suffering from the more acceptable malaria. (Unknown artist)

Some who had seen his eyes said they betrayed a certain madness. He was reputed to be a much-decorated war hero pensioned off on to prison camp duties after being driven mentally unstable by his experiences during the invasion of China. Whatever the truth of this, he was treated with great respect by all including, quite astonishingly, his Nip superiors. He stalked the camp carrying a thick bamboo pole used for administering instant justice to any prisoner who incurred his displeasure. Close on his heels padded his small squat interpreter, Kasi Yama, an oily character with a falsetto voice and a sly grin, who claimed to have learned his English at the Tokyo YMCA.

By this time considerable numbers of men were reporting sick, mainly with dysentery. Many were seriously ill. Even those not so badly affected were obviously unfit to join the airstrip working-parties. But the Bamboo Gunzo, as he quickly became known, wasn't going to have these walking sick loafing about the camp. He recruited them into working parties for so-called light duties. In fact they worked a damned sight harder than they would have done on the airstrip, digging drains around the huts and making roads. This improved camp conditions slightly, but it did nothing for the drain-diggers' health.

With alarming suddenness the semi-starvation that we had suffered since leaving Java began to take its toll. Our bodies offering little resistance, the spate of dysentery quickly grew into a disastrous epidemic. The first death, that of a Dutchman, came on the 12th. A Briton followed him on the 15th, and in the following 24 hours five more men died. News of the death of an eighth came as I sat writing in my diary that 790 of our 2075 men were now sick. Among them, predictably, was Bert, never by any stretch of the imagination fit enough to have set out for the islands at all. He lay in one of the huts the Nips ordered to be wired off from the rest of the camp as an isolation area. I crawled under the wire one night to see him, and found it hard to suppress a feeling of revulsion at the shrivelled caricatures of men lying wild-eyed on the bamboo shelves. For many the walk to the latrine trenches was out of the question. They had to just lie there in their filth hoping that an orderly might eventually come along to clean them up.

Of course there were no bedpans, but bamboo stems had been cut up into short lengths to use for urine. As I talked to Bert a man somewhere down the hut kept calling out "Bamboo, bamboo" to the almost non-existent orderlies. No-one came, and after a while the call changed to a reproachful "Too late, too late."

Bert was bearing up well, but felt extremely weak. I could do nothing to help. The doctors, with practically no medical supplies, were helpless. I crawled back under the barbed wire, despairing not only for Bert, but for all of us. Shortly afterwards I joined the swollen ranks of the sick in quarters. Nothing too serious. Just a recurrence of my malaria. But it came just in time to put me on the Gunzo's own special sick parade.

The Nips' first solution to the diminishing labour force had been to abandon the two-shift system on the airstrip and make everyone who could work, work twice as long. But soon comparatively few men remained fit for any sort of work at all.

The Gunzo found this situation totally unacceptable. So he ordered all the sick who were not in the isolation huts out on parade. Then he came stalking along the ranks examining his patients with his bamboo. Those he diagnosed as fit, which was almost everyone, he lashed with his pole and packed off to the airstrip.

Three dysentery victims in my line had collapsed under this treatment when the Gunzo reached me. Shivering under the tattered blanket round my shoulders, I muttered "malaria" and braced myself for a beating. None came. To my astonishment the Gunzo gave a sympathetic grunt and waved me unscathed back to my hut. It appeared that, while he despised anyone who had dysentery, malaria was a decent sort of illness that even your Samurai-type Nip could succumb to with honour.

Even the Gunzo's cure failed to bring any lasting increase in the men available for work, so the Nips tried another tactic. They doubled the rations of the men who went back to work on the airstrip and slashed those of the rest of the camp. The move won them at least one more worker, if not a very effective one. I shook off my malaria and joined the airstrip party.

It was very hot that first morning back at work, but around midday the storm clouds started gathering. Fortunately we had got what we had come for (the double ration of nasi goreng) before the typhoon struck. The downpour, driven by a violent wind, blotted out everything more than a few yards away. Soon water was a foot deep over the whole of our working area, and much deeper in the hollows. For two hours the Nips kept us going through the quite farcical motions of work, though we could only just manage to keep our balance against flood and wind. But at last even they had to admit defeat.

We struggled back to camp through raging torrent and storm débris. One man vanished when he misjudged where the track was beneath the flood and was completely submerged. Luckily he could swim and reached shallower water. As we approached the camp it became clear that structural damage was minimal, but the huts now stood in a quagmire. Worse still, the latrine trenches had overflowed and swarms of squirming maggots littered the paths.

With deaths now two or three a day it had become routine to inquire immediately on returning to camp whom we had lost during the day. Two more had gone, neither men I knew personally. But I was very concerned about Bert, and, taking advantage of the confusion caused by the storm, I crawled once more under the barbed wire into the isolation area to see him.

He had deteriorated sadly. He seemed quite oblivious to the storm or to much else going on around him. But one thing he was insistent on: that I should get out of that charnel house before I, too, became infected. After a short talk I gave way, and, shocked and not a little frightened at what I had seen, crept back to my side of the wire.

Our desperate need was an adequate diet, and there seemed not a hope of our getting it. Perhaps even the Gunzo realised this and, though he couldn't do much about it, he did make his own inimitable contribution.

A few nights later we were awakened in the early hours by the frenzied yelping of a dog somewhere close at hand. One or two of the more curious among us wanted to investigate, but guards around the huts stopped them going out. Then through the window spaces we saw a Nip come marching through the dripping nutmeg trees holding aloft a storm lantern. Behind him, in full uniform complete with sword, came the Gunzo. The lantern-bearer led the way towards the yelping. Then, as he raised his light even higher, we saw, swinging in the air, caught in the noose of a crude bamboo trap, one of the scrawny dogs we had seen at times scratching around the kampong. The Gunzo draw his sword and advanced. His blade flashed in the lamplight. The yelps turned to agonised howls as he nicked his helpless victim first on one side and then on the other. For a while he toyed with the dog like a cat with a mouse. Then, growing bored, he beheaded it with a single stroke. We shuddered and went back to an uneasy sleep.

That night there was dog stew on the menu. One emaciated pooch among 2000 may not seem very much, but we had developed such a craving for even a slight greasiness in our food that it was a red-letter day.

My next diary entry, for May 25, was written in one of the isolation huts. I had caught dysentery. Or, as I was too weak to catch anything, perhaps it would be more accurate to say it had caught me. Bert, sadly, had died the previous day. I was too ill to see him during his last days or even attend his burial. The death toll had begun to soar. It was now up to six or seven a day and the total exceeded fifty. The burials took place in a patch of semi-jungle just outside the barbed wire. The Nips would not allow wood to be used for coffins so our carpenters fashioned crude boxes out of strips of green bamboo. Working time was not to be wasted on funerals so they had to be held after dark. Here the Nips did make one concession. An officer in charge of a burial party was allowed a candle to illuminate the proceedings. Our officers tried to make it something like a funeral. Someone read a few words from the Prayer Book as a forlorn little group stood round in a shadowy, rather eerie circle. The presence of a duty Nip didn't help very much. He was there not to pay respect to the dead, but to keep a watch on the living. In fact on one occasion the Gunzo is reported to have appeared on the scene very drunk, only to vomit into the grave before it could be filled in.

As soon as I felt well enough I went to ask the medical orderlies what had happened to Bert's possessions. He had often shown me a gold pocket watch that had been presented to his father on retirement. He had prized it so much that he had refused to part with it even though its sale would have bought him some of the food he so desperately needed. I felt that some effort should be made to get it back to his widow. But the watch, along with the rest of his pathetic possessions, had vanished.

The orderlies had a dreadful job caring for dying dysentery patients, many of whom had lost control of their bodily functions. And whereas a man on the outside working party always had at least the hope that he might find or steal something more or less edible, the orderlies, confined within the camp, had no such opportunities. So if some came to regard a corpse's possessions as

Among the trees in the background hundreds died in unspeakable squalor. Haruku children fortunately ignorant of war pose in front of the site of the camp dysentery huts. (Dave Harries)

perks of the job it would be hard to judge them too harshly. There were always Nips ready to buy watches or rings. And with cash in hand you were ready to buy smuggled food when the opportunity presented itself.

In one case, I was told, orderlies divided a dying man's worldly goods just a little too early. He rallied sufficiently to realise what had happened and demanded them back. The problem was solved only when he had a relapse and finally moved on to where they were of no further use to him.

These matters shocked me profoundly at the time but, looking back, I feel that it was just a case of some of the orderlies realising sooner than most that ethics had to be modified in the battle for survival we were now facing. And if they found any way in which they could exploit their horrible job to improve their chances of staying alive they were going to take it.

A great morale-booster for us all at this time was the miracle of the four goats. So far as I knew these heaven-sent beasts amazingly arrived at the cookhouse quite out of the blue, to provide our first stew since Jaarmarkt in which you could actually see traces of flesh. It was only years later that I learned that the Nip commandant, in a moment of near humanity, had allowed three of our officers to go to the kampong to buy food, with their own money of course. At the time, apparently, he even went so far as to promise that such purchases could continue on a regular basis. But he quickly came to his senses and this gross deviation in Nip policy towards us was never repeated.

However, this was in no way surprising. The Nips themselves seemed to be having rations problems. We thought that perhaps supplies which should have reached Haruku were being sunk or commandeered by others along the supply line from Java. The island itself was geared to produce little more food than was necessary to feed its 500-odd population. It could hardly be expected to support the Nip garrison and 2000 prisoners.

The war had obviously brought great difficulties to the islanders themselves; nevertheless one or two of them took great risks to help us. As we struggled through the kampong, on our way to or from work, many a prisoner had a banana or a piece of sun-dried fish pressed into his hand. If the guards spotted the handover both giver and receiver were savagely beaten, and occasionally a native was left tied to a post along our route as a warning to others. Dialogue with the islanders was very restricted, but after we had had a few air-raid warnings and heard the sound of distant bombs they found a simple way to get over the message. "Americanos boom boom Ambon" told us all we wanted to know. The Nips eventually cut down fraternisation by building a new track to the airstrip, bypassing the kampong.

Meanwhile our death rate continued to rise and it began to dawn on the Nips that they were in danger of losing their entire labour force. Of course we didn't delude ourselves into thinking that the death of a couple of thousand British and Dutch would be of much concern to the Nips. As they never tired of telling us, they didn't believe in prisoners anyway. You fought and won or died honourably in the attempt.

But fortunately for us the Emperor, or one of his right-hand men, had decreed an airstrip on Haruku. To build it you needed labour. And in the remote and beleaguered Moluccas replacing two thousand coolies would be no easy matter. So the prisoners, or at any rate most of them, had to be kept alive, at least until the job was finished. It was time for drastic action. All work outside the camp, including even the hitherto sacrosanct airstrip party, was suspended so that we could concentrate on survival. And, so far as the Nips were concerned, no action could have been more drastic than that.

The camp itself was completely reorganised. Three separate sections were created and fenced off from each other, with movement between them strictly forbidden. Two were for the sick, a two-hut area for the dangerously ill and the dying, and a six-hut area for the rest of the dysentery cases, including me. Inside these two areas our hopelessly ill-equipped little band of British and Dutch doctors played a grim game of ludo, with their patients as the counters. The huts were numbered one to eight, and we were moved from one to the other according to the state of our health... to the bigger numbers if you improved, to the smaller numbers if you got worse. To be switched to Huts 1 or 2 amounted to a death sentence. Few came out alive. I was put in hut 4, strategically placed. I thought, for a move up or down.

9: HUT FOUR

June-July, 1943. Haruku, South Moluccas

Nights were the worst in the dysentery huts, particularly the dark draughty hours of tropical storms. You never slept long. Throughout the small hours an almost continual procession of half-dead men shuffled along the gangway between the sleeping shelves struggling to make it to the latrine. We judged our progress not by temperature or pulse, but by the number of trips we made to the bog. Some claimed to have clocked up an incredible 100 in 24 hours.

When the battering of the rain on the atap thatch eased off there came a reminder of many much worse off than those in Hut 4. Mingled with the distant howls of dogs in the kampong, came the cries of the delirious and dying in Huts 1 and 2.

Nevertheless, try as I might, I couldn't always resist the temptation to just lie there on my bamboo and rail against Fate for landing me up to my neck in the mire. But the more I thought about it the more I came to realise that it was not so much Fate as my efforts to frustrate her that were the cause of my predicament.

It had all started in 1938 with ugly rumours that all we young chaps were to be called up for national service. I didn't believe there was going to be a war and I didn't fancy this unwarranted interference with my life. So, instead of leaving the matter in Fate's good hands, I joined the RAFVR. That way I hoped to get away with no more damage than a spot of weekend training and annual camps. The result of my scheming was that I was called up and found myself full-time in the RAF a week before war had even been declared.

My next blunder came in late 1940 when I was quietly looking for "badges, cap, airmen for the use of" and the like at RAF Catterick. RAF Records posted LAC Peacock to Singapore, but Fate, in the shape of a friendly officer i/c stores, stepped in and offered to stop my move. No doubt he felt I was making far too great a contribution to the war effort in Europe to be wasted on the Far East. I would have none of it. Why should I give up this chance to see the mysterious Orient? Didn't I have a Chinese penpal to visit in Singapore? In January, 1941, I sailed from Liverpool on convoy J32/G. It was not until the early hours of December 8 that I realised what a mistake that was. I was rudely wakened by bombs bursting around my barrack block at RAF Seletar: the Nips' idea of a declaration of war.

By this time my ineptitude at controlling my life should have been apparent even to me. But unfortunately not. One of the perhaps less dramatic moves the RAF made to stem the Nip tide that was soon engulfing Malaya was the formation of No 1 Motor Transport Repair Section. My unit, Aircraft Depôt Far East, was to supply this select little band with a storebasher, and this lucky man was to be promoted to corporal.

The powers that be, who perhaps had even more important things on their minds at the time, gave the job to a chap straight out from Blighty who hadn't even got his knees brown. This was manifestly unfair to the old sweats, and the senior old sweat, I, was persuaded to protest. This was my biggest mistake. I got the job and made certain of a place behind the Nip barbed wire. Fate evacuated the chap I'd swapped jobs with safety to India. But no use blaming Fate. I'd made my bamboo shelf: now I had to lie on it.

Perhaps my best hope now was to try a little quiet prayer. I didn't see that it would make much difference. No listening, caring God could conceivably have allowed the slaughter and misery now afflicting his wartorn planet. But a few words couldn't do any harm. And let's not forget Allah and Buddha too, just in case. Pity the Hindu pantheon is so complex. It might be dangerous to invoke the wrong deity.

I returned to watching, with a sort of numbed detachment, the bizarre scene around me. Nearby a group of recovering patients squatted on the bamboo holding hands of unbelievably grubby playing cards close to their chests in a macabre game of bridge. They scarcely looked up from their bidding as the prisoner from the next sleeping place was carried off to death row. On the opposite bamboo a couple of men–about–camp, in filthy, ragged, lice-infested sarongs, discussed volubly the great meals of their lives. Their reminiscences came to a sudden stop when an exasperated involuntary listener threatened to kick their teeth in if they didn't shut up.

Occasionally a couple of prisoners with tanks strapped to their backs would come marching down the gangway, spraying the hut, and often the odd prisoner too, with disinfectant. These were newly-recruited medical orderlies. Very important persons these, because, as one of their duties was to bring food from the cookhouse, they had become the only prisoners allowed to move between the sick areas and the third section of the camp, that for the shrinking number of relatively fit men. With the food, they brought in news of the great big world outside the dysentery enclosures, all the latest absurd rumours. And, if you had generous friends on the outside, perhaps these orderlies might be bribed to bring you in a bit of coconut or a few tobacco leaves.

Fortunately, eager as the Nips claimed to be to die for their Emperor, this didn't seem to include dying of disease, so we didn't see a lot of them in the sick area. But we were accorded a sort of

Ex-prisoners who made a recent pilgrimage to Haruku found beef at the cookhouse at long last. This photo by Dave Harries shows fellow-pilgrim Tony Cowling with new-found friends on the cookhouse site. Cows now drink at the stream where prisoners drew water, washed themselves and did their laundry native-fashion

royal visit from the Gunzo and his shadow, Kasi Yama, now more generally referred to as Blood and Slime, those being the more obvious symptoms of dysentery.

News of their arrival spread consternation along the bamboo shelves, but the Gunzo quickly made it known through his interpreter that there was nothing for us to worry about. He had come, he asserted, out of concern for our welfare, to explain to us as a friend that, if we wanted ever to see our wives and sweethearts again, we had to get off the bamboo and go out to work. This unfortunately was no more than the truth. In the long run if you wouldn't, or simply couldn't, go out and work you were not going to survive. That was the cruel fact of life in Haruku. And while the wasted bodies carried out of the camp each night bore grim witness to the fact that few had any choice in the matter, there were some who, sick of the misery and hopelessness of it all, seemed to simply lie down and die.

But the Gunzo was on a morale-boosting campaign, trying to make light conversation, even to smile, but the distorted mouth beneath the inevitable dark glasses made him look grotesque rather than genial. The London newspapers, he suggested happily, would one day say he was a bad man. Perhaps he would have been hurt to know that even when he was subsequently hanged for war crimes the London newspapers remained completely indifferent.

For one of the sick at least the Gunzo was not all bad. This was an Englishman who, against all the odds, had fought his way back from Hut 1 to Hut 4. When the Gunzo heard of this achievement he made the lucky man a presentation of half a dozen sun-dried fish, which in Haruku was something like coming up on the treble chance.

As another part of the morale-boosting campaign the Nips produced 94 letters, the first mail we had even heard about since becoming prisoners. Many were for men who had died or who had never been in the camp anyway. Almost all had been posted in South Africa or India. There were only one or two from Britain and nothing for me, but surprisingly I was not too disappointed. Home had become a never-never land totally unconnected with the reality of Haruku.

What we needed to boost our morale was something to eat. In the isolation area the rations consisted of pap three times a day, flavoured at night with a little greasy water. Men in Huts 1 and 2

Gunzo Mori visited dysentery patients, like the prisoner in this Imperial War Museum picture, and explained as 'a friend' that if they ever wanted to see their wives and sweethearts again they had to get off the bamboo and go to work

received only water that rice had been cooked in.

Outside, the comparatively few fit men were now doing rather better. Nothing, it seemed, could change the ritual morning pap, but they fed on nasi goreng for lunch and, at night, steamed rice and a little stew which sometimes even contained traces of meat.

The Gunzo made sure he got value for the rich delicacies being provided by bullying and beating better roads and drains out of the recipients. But it did mean that they no longer needed to go on a jungle safari to get to the cookhouse.

Towards the end of the month the death rate began to slow down. The Nips decided they had stopped the rot. On June 1 they restarted outside working parties by sending a hundred men back to the airstrip.

June 3, however, brought a grim reminder that our troubles were not yet over. A storm at night deluged the camp. And as we shivered, damp and cold beneath the leaking roofs, eight more died. The death toll rose to 103.

On nights like this the camp became a veritable hell. And yet when the storm eased and the moon broke through the clouds to glint on the waving fronds of the coconut palms it brought a bizarre touch of magical beauty.

At last I was moved to a recovery hut. Here the ration had been revised to include a spoonful of vegetable soup with the midday and evening pap. And, astonishingly, there was also the occasional banana or even a bit of dried fish. By June 9, when the death toll had risen to 130, it was evident that dysentery was no longer the main killer. It was now starvation-related disease that was claiming lives.

Almost everyone in the isolation area had beri-beri. Some became horribly bloated with fluid, others grotesquely emaciated. Some men appeared to be going blind, others deaf. Some were partly paralysed. Blowflies laid their eggs in helpless patients' most vulnerable parts. Gaping tropical ulcers just wouldn't heal. Lice and bed bugs proliferated.

The Nips chose not to believe that we were starving, so our doctors carried out a post-mortem on one of the victims to illustrate the point. The body, according to the camp grapevine, was completely lacking in fat except for a small patch around the heart. Needless to say, the Nips simply ignored the findings.

Uneasy about my personal fat content, I crawled under the

barbed wire into the workers' area one night to try to scrounge some protein. I didn't find anyone very helpful. I was feeling much better by this time. I was still very weak but I realised that I was going to be even weaker if I didn't do something about it. The seaward side of the camp was unguarded, and it was possible to get down to the shore from the isolation area unobserved. I explored the possibilities of fishing. There were a few tiny hermit crabs that might provide bait. But standing on the narrow beach dangling a strand of sisal fibre and a bent pin over the incoming waves didn't really seem likely to bring in the rich harvest of the sea.

I decided I would do better to eat the bait. I managed to find a few dozen hermit crabs, but they were so tiny that when I had prised them from their winkle-like shells I had little more than a teaspoonful. I cooked, or at any rate burned them, over a fire in the hut. It was rather like eating gravel, but I got them down, convinced that they must contain some valuable protein.

The Nips put on pressure to get more men working on the airstrip. It was up to our doctors to keep up a supply of men miraculously cured from the recovery huts. We were called out on parade daily, immediately after the morning rice, each man holding out on a leaf in front of him his latest stool specimen. Excreta decided your immediate future.

If it were fairly solid the Dutch doctor would cajole: "A leetle light verk on ze aerodrome and I geev you pisang (banana)." And off you went to hack at coral on the airstrip. If, on the other hand, your specimen was watery you were assured of another twenty-four hours in the isolation area.

If the word on the grapevine was that outside rations were up and beatings down, there was quite a rush to get out. After all, our only long-term hope of survival lay in being where the food was. So if you couldn't supply a satisfactory stool of your own you had to buy one, perhaps with the banana you were hoping the doctor would give you. If, on the contrary, they reported life tough outside, the solid stool merchants not only found themselves out of business, but they might have to buy a liquid stool to avoid being sent out themselves.

The bombing of nearby Ambon became more intense. Optimists comforted themselves with the fond hope that the Yanks were preparing to retake the islands. Others wondered just how far it was to the nearest Allied-held territory. But it was no more than an idle thought. Many felt we had slipped up in not taking our chances, no matter how remote, immediately after the Java surrender. Now, desperately weakened by hardship and starvation, it was absurd even to think of escape.

But just over the water in Amahai, apparently, someone did. News somehow leaked out to us that four Eurasians, speaking the local language perfectly and possessing a sound knowledge of the area, had vanished from the camp. We never heard whether they made it. All it meant to us was a full-scale tenko of body counts, leg counts and interminable numbering in Nip to make absolutely sure that we were all present, dead or alive. There was one other escape. A Nip soldier vanished after being beaten up for being drunk. Search parties sent out to find him or his body found nothing.

Since arriving in Haruku we'd heard very little of what was going on in the rest of the world. Either rumours had completely dried up, or everyone was too busy with the more urgent matter of day-to-day survival to pass them on. But on June 15 the biggest whopper so far swept the camp. The war in Europe was over, no less. The Nip MO said so. The camp commandant said so. Britain was bright with lights again. Hitler was in Moscow for a peace conference. We'd no grounds for disputing it. We were cut off from any reliable source of information. Oh how we would have liked to believe it! But simply daren't. We couldn't afford to build up hopes only to have them explode in our faces. We just speculated on how the end of the war in Europe would affect us, and what Adolf was having for dinner in the Kremlin.

By July this latest rumour had died like the rest of them. But the weather was distinctly drier. Deaths were down to one or two a day. We even had one day without a funeral. The buzz from outside the sick huts was that there was meat in the rations, for workers only.

On one sensational afternoon three bullocks were driven down to the cookhouse. True, nearly all the meat was shortly afterwards carried back out of the camp up to the Nip barracks, but sufficient remained to provide a feast by Haruku standards, though for workers only. There was nothing for the sick.

This finally convinced me that while perhaps there was not much future as a Nip coolie on the airstrip, there was certainly none at all as a sick prisoner. I produced a fairly satisfactory stool, took my bribe of two pisangs and left the isolation area for "a leetle light verk on ze aerodrome."

10: THE LEGGI QUEUE

July – September, 1943.   Haruku, South Moluccas

Little had changed when I returned to the airstrip working-party. The coral humps were still there. We still hacked at them ineffectively with our hammers and chisels and moved what débris we produced with our little baskets. The Nips were still there, encouraging us in their usual charming manner. The big event of the day remained the midday nasi goreng.

We all got a little edgy when it arrived. It was vital that, when the knocking-off bugle sounded, you were in as good a position as your job would allow for the race to the food queue. The prize for the winners was extra grub. For immediately the first man got his rice he moved to the opposite side of the food box to start the leggi queue. Leggi is a corruption of the Malay word, *lagi* meaning 'more'. And the distribution system was such that there was always more for those served first. The man with the most important job of the day was the server, who had to divide out his box of rice among perhaps fifty starving men. His tools comprised an old tin can to which a wooden handle had been attached, and a spatula. As we had no way of obtaining extra supplies, failing to make the rice go round would be a crime too horrendous to contemplate.

The server had to judge just how loosely or tightly to pack each scoopful to produce the required number of portions. He also had to ensure that all portions were the same. There were generally one or two self-appointed scrutineers on hand to see that he didn't pack the scoop extra tightly for his pals. His ideal would be to produce just one more scoopful than the number of men, for by tradition the server always went to the head of the leggi queue. Some developed surprising accuracy, but none would risk running short, so there was always leggi for some, including of course the server himself. In fact, with a nervous server, it was not unknown to have leggi for all and leggi leggi for those at the head of the queue. However it worked out, it was obviously more profitable

Prisoners wait anxiously for their rice at a five-star officers-only prison camp. But no doubt the battle for 'leggi' was just as intense, if a little more restrained, as on Haruku. (Imperial War Museum)

to devote one's energies to getting to the head of the rice queue rather than hacking coral.

Progress with the airstrip remained painfully slow. Painful to us. Slow to the Nips. So perhaps it was in an effort to increase productivity that the Nips re-introduced wages. As well as our board and lodging, we were to get ten cents a day, as in Semarang and Jaarmarkt.

Again this introduction of pay complicated a socio-economic system which, if nothing else, had been a model of simplicity. Again the Nips were paying out cash which, so far as their regime allowed, we had absolutely no way of spending.

This time they tried to do something about it. A little bamboo hut was erected on the square to house the camp shop. Mostly its shelves were bare, but every now and again supplies of local tobacco leaves, pisang and, on very rare occasions, dried fish were obtained from the kampong.

The shop opened, when it opened at all, immediately after the working parties had been counted and dismissed. The Nips intended to see that it was the workers who got the goodies. But prices were very high for ten-cents-day men and customers tended to be those who had made money in strictly illegal deals with natives or Nips, or by smuggling contraband into camp.

Faced with the sort of problem that no doubt sometimes baffles Chancellors of the Exchequer today, the Nips tried another way of channelling rewards to deserving mouths. No purchases were to be made without a special ticket issued only to workers. To qualify for one of these much-sought-after tickets you had to be on an outside working party at the time some sort of supplies turned up for the shop and, most important, while the Gunzo was in a generous frame of mind.

Whether or not there would be an issue of tickets became a burning issue of the working day. We even had a little song about it, sung to the tune of the Nips' lights-out bugle call. Unfortunately it is not fit to repeat. Of course the tickets didn't defeat the camp tycoons. They had more than enough cash to buy up the tickets as well as the tobacco.

Although most of us had long since realised all our saleable assets somewhere along the painful hungry road from sun-soaked Tasikmalaya to rain-sodden Haruku, there was the odd bod who had been slow to appreciate the absurdity of hanging on to a wedding ring or perhaps a last token from a girlfriend when its sale might make all the difference between starvation and survival. But the last trinkets were now on offer. The easiest and certainly safest way of selling was through an experienced dealer who had established some sort of understanding with his Nip counterparts. But naturally he would want a hefty cut. You could try to do the deal yourself, but there were snags. Not the least being that the Nips didn't always take too kindly to a refusal of their final offer.

I became painfully aware of this while on a Chinese wheelbarrow job with Sid, a particular friend of mine, who was still holding on to a gold wristwatch as a sort of last-ditch emergency fund and felt the safest place to keep it was on his wrist. Our boss for the day was the Mad Monk, a Nip who invariably appeared on working parties in a cowl, and boasted a smattering of English and a spiv's eye for any valuable he could pick up cheap. Watches were extremely rare by this time, so when the Monk saw Sid's he quickly got in an offer. We were humping boulders through a clump of sago palms with particularly vicious thorns. Each completed trip earned a token from the Monk in the shape of a pebble. Sid refused to sell, so the Monk kept us haggling instead of humping, not an unattractive alternative when sago thorns kept piercing the scraps of old rubber that passed for footwear. But at the end of the day came the reckoning. The Monk raised his eyebrows beneath his cowl as he looked at our pitiful collection of pebbles. Then he switched his eyes meaningfully to Sid's watch. It was obviously a case of sell or take a beating for slacking. And Sid wasn't selling. We took our punishment.

With the dysentery huts emptying and more men becoming available for outside work, parties were occasionally sent right out on the fringes of the airfield or even to other parts of the island. This opened up increased opportunities of smuggling tobacco or coconut oil back into camp. Hopefully, as you staggered along a track with your load of boulders or whatever, a native would materialise out of the surrounding bush ready to hand over a slab of the local weed, provided of course you had the cash to pay for it. And if you got your loot safely back into camp you could divide it into small portions and sell it to the nicotine addicts at an enormous profit. But it was risky. We often returned to camp to find the guards waiting to carry out a search. And punishment could be severe.

On one occasion we arrived back to find the Gunzo out on the square laying into two men with his bamboo. They had been caught redhanded with contraband. Instead of being dismissed, our party was split into two groups. One hundred of us were marched towards each offender and ordered to clout him across the face as we passed. The first few men tried to pull their punches, whereupon the Nips stepped in to clout both clouter and clouted. Before long the two men being punished were appealing to their comrades to hit them hard the first time to avoid bringing in the Nips. Badly bruised and rocked by each successive blow they stood their ground as the brutal spectacle continued.

Then the Gunzo, in an effort to inflame us against his victims, stunned us with the worst possible blow for starving men. The whole camp was to be denied its evening meal. But he was up against two hard-as-nails Palestinians. And one of them, though scarcely able to keep on his feet, begged that he should have extra punishment so that the camp could have its food. At this the Gunzo, impressed by this astounding display of guts, relented and ended the whole miserable spectacle.

The camp entrepreneurs were somewhat subdued that night, but they still went off to work next morning with cash hidden in their water bottles and high hopes of a big deal.

We all went off to work every day full of hope. Hope that we might find some edible weed along the track, hope that we might get the chance to steal something from some unfortunate native's veg patch, hope that we might get through the day without a kick in the guts.

By this time we had learned from our Dutch Eurasian companions what wild plants, roots and fruits we could eat without poisoning ourselves, though mistakes did occur. The main problem was that our regular route to the airstrip had long since been stripped bare. You had to get away from the normal working areas to find anything worthwhile.

As for thieving, we had no scruples about taking anything from anyone except fellow prisoners. But opportunities were very few, and the haul unlikely to be more than a half-grown papaya as hard as a cannonball.

On July 20 we clocked up our 500th day in the bag, and confidently assured one another: "It won't be long now." After 500 days we thought we knew only too well the Nip attitudes to the death of a prisoner. So we were amazed at their reaction when a Dutchman was killed by a lorry on the airstrip. They pressured the natives into supplying proper hardwood for a coffin. From somewhere or other they conjured up flowers for a very presentable wreath. And a party of Nip officers and NCOs, spruced up in full uniform, paraded for the ceremony. It was as near to full military honours as could be expected on our fringe of the Emperor's empire.

Meanwhile, in a shack a few yards away, lay the bodies of the latest dysentery victims, swathed in scraps of filthy blanket, each with a stone on top to stop his identification slip blowing away. Like the 240 who had gone before them they waited for their bamboo suits and a perfunctory burial when the Nips found time for it.

It was how you died that mattered. A Nip showed us another way to qualify for the full treatment shortly after the Dutchman's funeral. He went out and shot himself, a nice clean honourable way of joining the ancestors.

Inspired by the dry weather and the increasing reservoir of labour at his disposal when the walking sick quit the dysentery huts and joined the inside working-parties, the Gunzo now emerged as a fanatical town planner and road builder. Encouraged by his bamboo pole his slave gangs demolished the isolation huts, turned the track down to the cookhouse into the best road on the island, and fashioned a vegetable garden out of the camp swamp.

But undoubtedly his greatest achievement was the sea-view superloo he had built out over the beach. For some time the Nips had resisted this rather obvious solution to the camp's sanitation problems, but at last a sturdy bamboo pier was erected, with a cross piece at the sea end punctuated with holes at appropriate intervals. The opening of this masterpiece was a great occasion for the Gunzo. He looked on with pride as the first customers arrived and crouched on their haunches over the holes like a troop of bare-bottomed monkeys. The British clutched bunches of leaves; the more practical Dutch each carried a bottle of water suspended from a finger with a piece of string. The Gunzo appeared to consider for a moment these primitive Western ideas of hygiene, then he strolled benignly along the line of squatting men presenting each with a square of Nip toilet paper. As he stood back to see his gifts put to good use, each man, British and Dutch alike, carefully folded up the precious piece of paper and stowed it carefully away. The British used their leaves; the Dutch their water. The Gunzo scratched his head and walked away. Every scrap of paper on the camp, including even the odd Bible, had been used to roll the local tobacco into cigarettes. Toilet paper was certainly much too valuable to be used on backsides. Unfortunately the sea-view loo, clean and free from insects and maggots, did not last very long. According to Kasi Yama it had to go because there was a danger that it might spread our diseases round the world.

Undeterred, the Gunzo redoubled his efforts to turn our slum into a garden suburb. He was supervising a gang of us on road improvement work one morning when a formation of a dozen four-engined bombers came roaring in from the sea at no more than six or seven hundred feet. He looked up casually, beamed with pride, and murmured "Nippon." A prisoner looked up too, and throwing discretion to the winds, or somewhere, put him wise. "Nippon no," he asserted. "Americano." There was an expectant hush. Then the Gunzo, realising the awful truth, leapt on to the pushbike he used for touring his realm, and went belting across the island brandishing his sword at the fast-disappearing aircraft.

Some time later he came cycling dejectedly back. And as the rumble of bombs was heard in the distance he flung his sword on the ground. Perhaps that gesture summed up the Gunzo. He was a sort of Genghis Khan character stranded in the wrong century.

But our samurais were beginning to learn a thing or two as the war crept nearer to Haruku. When they arrived in Java they had scoffed at our air-raid shelters. They were not afraid to die, they boasted, as they kept us busy filling them in. But now, on our little island, excavations were starting everywhere. We were allowed to dig our own shelters alongside our huts, and surprised even ourselves with the unexpected reserves of energy we found when working for our own self-preservation.

Meanwhile a Nip camouflage team draped the camp barbed wire with palm leaves. This sparked off long discussions as to whether it was to our advantage that our camp be recognised from the air. One school of thought believed it certainly was and that the Nips were just making sure we got bombed along with everyone else. Others thought the last thing the bomb-aimers were going to worry about was a bunch of Pows working for the Nips, and our best hope was to pretend to be coconuts. One thing we noticed was that our jailers were getting very edgy. We could understand their strengthening the camp guard, but we felt they were going a bit over the top, even for Nips, when they started looking for a spy.

This bizarre development was brought rudely to our attention when work on the airstrip was stopped and we were all lined up for an identity parade. It appeared that an ambitious native informer had persuaded some gullible Nip that he had seen a prisoner pass a message to a native. What sort of message, we never knew. Perhaps a coded signal to armed accomplices outside that we would strangle our guards at midnight and seize control of the island.

Whatever it was, the Nips took it all seriously and the informer was conducted along the ranks of pathetic, starving wrecks to unmask his 007. Each of us waited fearfully as this phony spy-spotter passed along the rows. He must have become pretty desperate himself as he scrutinised face after face without finding anyone remotely likely for the rôle.

He had obviously got himself into a position where offering up even the most unlikely spy was better than no spy at all. The Nips had to have their man. So from the last row he singled out a frail innocuous RAF corporal. His unfortunate victim was immediately seized by the guards, marched back to camp and slung in the guardroom. And shortly afterwards came the grim announcement that he was to be shot at nine o'clock that night.

The whole camp was stunned by the news. We faced many hazards and had grown to accept them, but to shoot a man on such a phony charge as this was cheating even by Nip rules and regulations. And unless the position of the new camp latrines was a military secret none of us had any information to pass on to anyone anyhow. Our officers were stung into action. At no little risk to themselves they presented a petition to the camp commandant calling for the corporal's immediate release. This didn't do a great deal to raise our hopes as their efforts on our behalf had proved singularly ineffective in the past.

But this time the Nips confounded us. According to the camp grapevine the Gunzo and the camp commandant went so far as to back the petition. It was rushed off, so rumour had it, to the island governor, a dignitary of whose existence we had so far been totally unaware.

We waited anxiously as the minutes ticked on towards execution time. Then, as suddenly and surprisingly as he had been arrested, the corporal was freed, just in time for supper. What happened to the informer we never knew, but his prospects didn't seem bright.

August came, and with it the Glorious Twelfth, Pow version, not grouse shooting, but louse hunting. For some time I had been pestered by small, itchy bumps which had begun on my hands and gradually spread to other parts of my body. They were not only extremely irritating but induced a depressing feeling of uncleanliness that no amount of washing could erase. This scabies, spread by lice, travelled through the camp like bad news. Fortunately this was one of the few complaints for which our doctors were able to produce effective treatment. And as soon as we were able to get a day off work they started the cure.

First we all paraded naked and greased ourselves from head to foot in a mixture of coconut oil and sulphur. This had to stay on for a very sticky 24 hours. Then we took all the clothing and bedding we possessed out into the sun and carried out one great simultaneous louse hunt.

Of course we had all carried out innumerable individual louse hunts before, but they were of limited use when a new army of lice was waiting to move in from the bloke next door. And they were armies. One chap, partially blinded by the sun, claimed that he first realised he was lousy when he noticed the pattern on his blanket changing its shape.

The next phase of the decontamination operation was to batter the round brown bugs out of the bamboo slats we slept on. The camp was soon reeking of the incense-like odour they gave off when crushed. It was a little trying to put up with the loathsome mixture of sweat, coconut oil and sulphur for the necessary twenty-four hours, but it did the trick. And how exhilarating it felt to be released for a while from scabies, lice and bedbugs!

A full moon in early September brought American bombers over our island almost nightly. They came in from the east, and then, as the droning died away, we lay on our bamboos silent and expectant, listening for the thunder as they dropped their load somewhere on or around Ambon. Shortly afterwards they returned, homeward bound, often flying low and clearly visible in the bright moonlight. We speculated on what gargantuan feast awaited the crews at their bases.

With the war around us hotting up, the Nips were beginning to need our airstrip badly. Though blasting had now superseded the farcical hammer-and-chisel approach, we still had a long way to go and felt in no hurry to get there. I can't honestly claim that we were purposely hindering the Nip war effort, but realised that the bombers would no longer be paying us merely social calls once the island had an operational airstrip.

The Nips, who, I suspect, had never been taught that patience is a virtue, became increasingly frustrated, and reacted true to form. Where ten men weren't getting the desired result they shoved in twenty. We all got in one another's way and slow became dead slow. The Nips moved in, punching and kicking indiscriminately, with frenzied shouts of "Kanairo" and "Bugairo": we were never offered a precise translation, but we got the general idea. Dead slow became full stop.

The explosive situation was eventually defused with a few

second-hand bombs. These bombs, bequeathed to the Nips by the Dutch along with their East Indian empire, were buried in the obstinate coral and exploded. Contrary to our expectations no-one was killed or maimed, and the job took a giant leap forward.

Surprisingly quickly the airstrip's demand for coolie labour eased and more and more of us worked on other sites around the island where often the pace was easier and the foraging prospects more favourable. Gangs tended to go off in the same order each morning, so we could predict which part of the parade would go where. This resulted in a rugby scrum as we jostled one another for positions in the ranks we thought might avoid the airstrip and get us a softer or more lucrative job elsewhere. This puzzled the Nips for a while, but not for long. When they tumbled what was going on they took to reversing the whole parade so that no-one went where he had hoped.

Meanwhile, despite rumours to the contrary, that other war, somewhere on the other side of the world, still rumbled on. We now heard that Italy had surrendered and Hitler was rushing troops over the Brenner Pass. We treated this story like the rest of the hogwash constantly being slung at us. This report, the odd one out, was quite true. But we had been told so many lies that we couldn't believe anything.

We concentrated on the more important things in life. A crocodile and three water buffalo materialised at the cookhouse. A Eurasian friend caught two eels in the stream and invited me to help him eat them.

Then came a really big event. A supply ship arrived off the island, and I found myself in a hopeful band of men being marched off to the jetty to unload it. Who knew what goodies might just happen to fall off the back of a prisoner? The ship, of perhaps some 3000 tons, was much too big to come in to the landing, and anchored about half a mile out. We were loaded in sampans to go out to her. No matter: the bigger the ship, the bigger the cargo.

Our first suspicion that the job might not be all it seemed came when the Nips in the sampan with us asked, with the help of a bit of arm-waving, how many of us could swim. It seemed an idle question. We didn't need to swim to bring in the rice, meat, and goodness knew what other delicacies the ship might have in her hold. But, as they had asked, no, none of us could swim. We hadn't much pride left, but we felt insulted by the implication that we were mad enough to volunteer as shark bait. The Nips fell silent.

Then, as we neared the ship, the awful truth dawned. Her cargo was not food, but petrol. Sailors began dropping drums of it into the sea, and our Nips indicated that, swimmers or non-swimmers, we had to dive in after it. The job on which we had pinned such high hopes would be to propel the drums into shore. We weren't tremendously enthusiastic, particularly those who really couldn't swim. But with a little gentle persuasion we took off our shorts and jumped, or were pushed, over the side. Eventually, encouraged by the yells of the Nips, we all found ourselves a drum, and, hanging on for dear life by our arms and kicking out frantically with our legs, we got our little petrol armada on course for dry land.

The beach seemed a long way off, and we soon found we had a strong cross-current to contend with. We began drifting away along the coast. The Nips made for the shore in the sampan, leaving us on our own. One Captain Cook among us did suggest heading for Australia, but the rest of us landlubbers were too busy navigating to a nice dry prison island to heed him.

At length we realised that current and tide were taking us inshore anyway, and we coasted along to ground, after a voyage of an hour or so, on a completely deserted golden beach. We had barely touched bottom, however, when our squad of Nips, who had presumably calculated our landfall, appeared out of the undergrowth. And soon twenty naked men, feeling more than a little vulnerable without their shorts, were straining to push their barrels up a steep beach, goaded on by a bunch of grossly overdressed guards.

We stacked the drums quickly and neatly. You don't invite aggro when you're in your birthday suit. Then we set out on the shortest route we hoped, back to our shorts. The Nips, however, decided our path lay through a small kampong, and I feel sure that some grannies on Haruku to this day still talk of the time a score of naked white men came marching into their village. Their menfolk were all away, presumably working for the Nips, and the terrified women fled into the bush sending cooking-pots flying in all directions as they scattered.

11: DOUBLE ANNIVERSARY

September – December, 1943. Haruku, South Moluccas

By the end of September my dysentery recurred and I found myself back in the isolation area. Although there were now far fewer huts and the grounds had been tidied up, some things had not changed. I was just in time for yet another of the periodic purges against the sick. Rations were cut, any attempts at private cooking banned. We were even stopped from going down to the sea, no small hardship when the only other washing-place, the camp stream, lay on the other side of barbed wire which fenced us off from the so-called fit men.

Our spirits did not greatly improve after a visit to our huts from Kasi Yama. This time he did not come trailing at the heels of the Gunzo: perhaps he was trying to prove to us, or maybe to himself, that he was not merely his master's yap dog. His message, however, remained familiar. If we insisted on remaining obstinately ill, we could stay put and die. If we hoped ever to see England again, we must get out of hospital and work hard.

Then on September 30, as though to emphasise the fact that we, the sick, had been abandoned, came the news of extra rations and a day off work for those on the other side of the wire. The first planes, three light twin-engined jobs, had made a triumphant landing on our airstrip. It was time to celebrate. Up to then the project had cost 315 prisoners' lives.

On October 5, as I lay on the bamboo, ill and depressed, a food carrier rushed into the hut to tell us that a second batch of mail had arrived on the camp, this time from England. An officer who had helped to sort it had made a list of the names. The food carrier read them out, among them mine.

Of course the Nips did not release the mail immediately. They were doing us a great favour in letting us have our letters at all. Such generosity could be justified only when they felt we were adequately fulfilling our rôle as obedient slaves and the Americans

111

were not sinking too many Nip aircraft carriers.

So we waited. But, strangely, although I'd had no word from my family for nearly two years, this pin-pricking didn't bother me much. Home seemed to be in another existence at another time, difficult to relate to my real world on Haruku. Memories of my old life had become blurred as I concentrated on keeping alive.

When, a couple of days later, the letters were released, I went to collect mine without much emotion. But, as I recognised my mother's handwriting on the envelope, suppressed emotions raced to the surface. I realised with a jolt how much I missed home and how much anguish my absence must be causing there.

The letter had been written just after the fall of Java, eighteen months ago, before my family knew I was a prisoner and before the Nips had decreed that any communication with prisoners should be in dehumanised block capitals on brief postcards. The

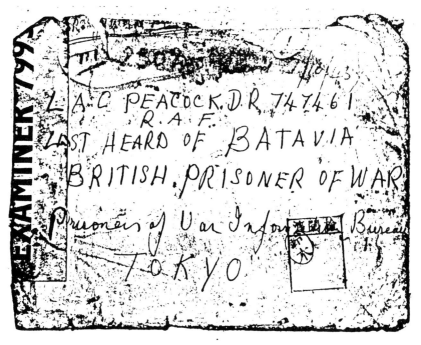

The envelope that brought a tear to the author's eye. Amazingly this despairing address was enough to find him some eighteen months later half a world away in Haruku. And it didn't even have a stamp on it

poignant, despairing address, "Last heard of Batavia," in the familiar handwriting brought a tear to my eye.

Back on my bamboo I indulged in a little self-pity. But bemoaning my luck was going to get me nowhere. What Kasi Yama said was right. I was one of the lucky ones, lucky enough to be able to take the little bastard's advice. On October 20 I rejoined the workers.

By this time the camp backroom boys (Dutch who knew the local flora and our more botanically-minded doctors) were working on Project Kedley Bean. How this nutritional wonder arrived on the camp I don't know. Perhaps it just turned up with the green leaves and was about to be slung in the stew when some alert genius spotted it.

Under the supervision of our boffins these precious beans were put to soak. A few of the walking sick were given a crash course in kedley stomping, and spent long hours dancing on the submerged beans until the beans were battered into submission. They were then stacked on shelves and left to acquire a greyish mould. After a few days they were pronounced to have transformed themselves into tempe, crawling with vitamins and God knew what else, and ready to eat. And that was not all. Another batch of these versatile beans was ground to a powder, mixed with moderately clean water and left to mature as kedley milk, far richer, they assured us that anything mere cows could produce.

The milk benefitted the seriously ill. All of us got a little tempe in turn. And if the beans weren't life-savers, we believed they were, which was almost as good.

Another pick-me-up came from the Nips themselves. They issued verbally what amounted to their first unofficial bulletin on the war around Ambon. One of their pilots, they claimed, had singlehandedly sunk 14 out of 15 ships attacking the island. He had then run out of bombs and ammo. But did this heroic Nip regard this as an excuse for slinking back to his base? Not on your life. He crashed his plane on the 15th ship and sank that as well. Needless to say this newsflash didn't have quite the effect the Nips had presumably intended.

The Gunzo, not generally a bundle of laughs, also raised a smile. In one of his all too frequent sullen and unpredictable moods (we thought he was affected by the moon) he entered into some sort of dispute with the Nip MO. We scattered as the MO came racing through our huts pursued by a ferocious Gunzo waving a revolver. The younger and fitter MO made it to his own hut and locked himself in. The frustrated Gunzo put three shots through the hut door before abandoning the hunt. This little break in the humdrum camp routine was enjoyed by prisoners and Nips alike, with the exception, presumably, of the MO.

On November 17 the Nips started sending off small parties of prisoners by sampan to work in Ambon. Within three days a total of 150 men had left in this way. Then, on November 23, 650 of the sick received 24 hours' notice to be ready to leave for Ambon to join a ship, so the Nips said, bound for Java. With an air-raid warning on the aerodrome and the sound of AA fire over Ambon, they left fearfully, looking forward to the comparative luxury of Java, but wondering if they'd ever arrive there.

At no time so far had we noticed our hosts going overboard with comforts for the troops, so it came as a surprise when half a dozen Nip women appeared on the island. Perhaps it was a surprise for the Nip authorities too, because no accommodation had been prepared for the new arrivals. However two or three days' enthusiastic building in the kampong produced a house that was quite palatial by Haruku standards. And in no time at all the brothel was in business, just in time for the double anniversary.

Although Pearl Harbour was blitzed on December 7 it was already December 8 in Tokyo, on the other side of the international dateline. So the Americans marked the Day of Infamy the day before the Nips celebrated their "glorious victory," an anomaly which cost us the day off the Nips had promised us for the great occasion.

The morning of the seventh was dull and mainly overcast as we pretended to work on the airstrip. I heard a shout, and looked up to see bombers diving towards us out of the cloud. There was a general stampede. With no sort of cover anywhere near, it was just a matter of getting as far away as possible as quickly as possible.

Prisoners who, seconds earlier, had been dragging themselves around as though the next step might be their last, were miraculously galvanised into greyhounds. We'd left the protesting Nips well behind when the earth began to heave and everyone fell flat. For a minute or two we lay there petrified, our ears numbed by the horrendous thunder. Then, realising the danger had passed leaving us unscathed, we rose slowly to our feet. Everything seemed

So peaceful now in this Dave Harries picture, but on December 7, 1943, a squadron of bombers came plummeting out of the clouds above this jetty and blasted the village in the background. Prisoners spent December 8 searching the smouldering ruins for bodies

pretty much unchanged except that clouds of thick smoke began to rise over the sea end of the runway.

The guards herded us back on the job. The Gunzo came steaming up on his bike, showing touching concern for his subjects. We resumed work, keeping a watch on the sky and straining our ears for the sound of aircraft. Slowly, scraps of information about the raid began to trickle through to us. The bombs had dropped on the kampong and a Nip barracks as well as the airstrip. We had not got off scot free. One prisoner had been killed, another badly injured and half a dozen others less seriously hurt. The Nips had lost three soldiers at the barracks and one of the newly-arrived brothel girls.

But by far the worst hit were the natives, mere bystanders in a war brought to their island by foreigners. Bombs presumably aimed at the airstrip had fallen short and demolished their village instead. The men were out working so it was their families who perished as their flimsy houses were burned down or reduced to rubble. About fifty had died, nearly all women or children.

Next day, the glorious eighth, which was to have been our day off, we were marched off to the kampong. The ruins stank with the nauseating smell of burnt flesh. We were set to work looking for bodies and generally clearing up. One tearful native begged my little group to search for his wife among the débris of a house. It soon became quite obvious that there was no-one there, but, in response to his entreaties we continued sweating among the charred wreckage. Then, suddenly, he grabbed a bundle of notes from a hole in the ground beneath a beam we had moved, and scuttled off, his grief considerably relieved.

I had mixed feelings about the air-raid. On the one hand it provided encouraging confirmation that the Americans were now knocking hell out of the Nips in our vicinity. On the other hand it not only emphasised the increasing danger of staying on the island, but raised fears about the prospects of getting safely off it. Though we had more or less finished the job we had been sent to do, there was not much danger of our becoming redundant. The air-raid inspired a sudden demand for air-raid shelters at the Nip barracks.

We spent our second Christmas Day in the bag digging air-raid shelters. But we weren't complaining. The Nips had played Santa and given us what seemed at the time the most useful present we could have wished for, a day off and permission to dig bigger and deeper dug-outs around our huts.

That took care of our day's entertainment. All that remained was the little matter of our Christmas dinner. And by the routine expedient of saving a portion of our rations daily over the previous week our cooks were able to dish up enough for us to stuff ourselves fairly adequately on the big day. We told each other we'd be home for our next Christmas, thanked our lucky stars that we were still alive, and strengthened our resolve to keep it that way.

Over the next two days the 150 men who had been sent to work on Ambon trickled back to Haruku by sampan. We listened eagerly to their story because it was the only first hand information we received from the outside world during our stay on the island. They had visited the town of Ambon and confirmed that it had been damaged by air-raids. But most of the bombing, they said, had been directed at shipping in the island's vast natural harbour.

The object of their trip had been to bolster up the labour force at Liang, an airstrip similar to our own. They had been billeted at a Pow camp on its perimeter, a camp structurally just like ours: same leaky atap huts, same barbed wire. But there was one big difference. The Haruku officers (all the British were RAF) had had their authority over the other ranks completely undermined by the Nips. They had some privileges. They had their own hut. They had even managed to hang on to two or three batmen. But, doctors apart, they were, in the Haruku scheme of things, largely redundant. Their functions for the most part were taken over by the Nips, while they were reduced to acting as Aunt Sally foremen on working-parties.

The doctors had the hopeless, never-ending task of trying to cope with a mammoth sick list with virtually nothing in the way of medical supplies or facilities.

The officers may have bemoaned the fact that traditional service discipline – the saluting, jankers and all the rest of the bull – had long been forgotten. But this created surprisingly few problems, and the fact that we were no longer so many officers and men, but more fellow-prisoners with one common enemy, created a friendly atmosphere between ranks which more than compensated for the slavish obedience which had been lost.

The Liang Pows were largely Army and their officers had retained control of internal discipline. They had remained, so our friends from Liang told us, officers first and foremost. They had even gone so far as to hold courts-martial and (this really stuck in our friends' gullets) had facilities for handing the guilty over to the Nips for punishment in the Nip cells. There appeared to be three sides in the daily battle. The men had not only the Nips to contend with, but still faced the old familiar confrontation with the officers. And our friends thought this a high price to pay for having an Army bugler sound the Last Post at your funeral. However, it must be said, Liang at this time had lost 80 men out of the original 1000, which compared very favourably with Haruku.

Buglers apart, Liang burials were no less primitive than our own. On one occasion, for instance, the Nips, after refusing even a bit of bamboo for the coffin, reprimanded the officer in charge of the bearers for returning without the filthy torn piece of blanket the body had been wrapped in. Sadly we learned that twenty-one of the sick who had left Haruku for Ambon had ended up no farther than Liang, and one of them had died while our 150 men

117

were there.

One encouraging snippet from our Liang contingent was that it had been possible at some time to get a chicken on the camp black market. Of course it was for millionaires and camp racketeers only, but it was great news to us in Haruku that the chicken was not extinct. It was with enormous relief that we saw out 1943. We prayed to all the gods we could think of for better times to come in 1944.

12: KING OF HARUKU

January – May, 1944. Haruku, South Moluccas

We began 1944 with a day off and a cable from the Red Cross. A Nip solemnly read it out on parade. It said that the International Red Cross sent its greetings to all prisoners of war. End of message. I don't think the idea that such a thing as a Red Cross parcel could reach Haruku ever occurred to us. But we took some encouragement from the fact that the Nips had recognised that the Red Cross existed. Above all we started the year with a new optimism, gathering evidence all around us that the war was at last going our way. This brought its problems, but we dug our slit trenches a little deeper and hoped for the best. After all our troubles, we felt we just had to survive now.

The Nips, too, seemed to have survival uppermost in their minds. They transferred large sections of the outside working parties on to a feverish shelter-building campaign at the island's main barracks. They were spurred on by the almost daily drone of large formations of American bombers and the not-too-distant thunder of bursting bombs. A raid on the night of the January 11-12 lasted two and a half hours. Rumours, on which we still lived, had it that twenty-two ships had been sunk.

So I found myself playing a humble part in the construction of the Odeon, architectural wonder of Haruku. It started out simply enough as a pit dug six feet deep in the coral. Then, as the Nips were a bit short of reinforced concrete and armour plating, we cut down a grove of coconut trees. Next, encouraged by a vintage display of shouting and kicking by the guards, we assembled the trunks into three rafts and set them at right angles to each other over the hole. In a frenzied session with our Chinese wheelbarrows we covered the palms with more and yet more earth. Then came the final touch of technological genius. As a sort of crowning glory we erected over the pinnacle of this twentieth century pyramid a small bamboo platform. This, we gathered, was

119

intended to explode the bomb before it hit the main edifice. I never experienced how it felt to be in the shelter during an air raid, but it scared the living daylights out of me to go down into it at any time.

The worst part of the shelter-building lark was carrying the coconut trunks around on our shoulders. It looked oh so easy when we saw a group of natives gaily trotting along with the load balanced evenly between them, but very different when we tried to put it into practice. Somehow that perfect synchronisation, that certain poetry of motion, seemed to be lacking. And there were some anxious moments when one of the four or five men on the tree mistimed that vital hoist on to the shoulders, or the even more crucial heave to get rid of the brute.

Being on the short side, I could sometimes walk fairly comfortably in the middle of a gang with the tree held more or less clear of my shoulder by taller men in front and at the rear. Unfortunately the island tracks made no pretence at being level and every so often the tree came crashing down on to me as I reached the top of a hump while those in front of and behind me were on lower ground.

The more frenzied the Nips became about their shelters, the wilder the rumours grew. We even had the Nips asking the Allies for surrender terms. Perhaps we invented this ourselves to take our minds off the food situation, which had now reached an all-time low. It seemed that supply ships were just not getting through to the island. We were down to a little rice, kedley beans and a few green leaves from our garden. We called them our gardens though in fact we didn't derive much benefit from them, once the Nips had taken what they wanted.

Perhaps it was the food problem (we hoped it was their military situation) but something inspired the Nips at this point to issue what was perhaps their most surprising order of the day. They told us we were to pray for one minute each morning and evening. They didn't specify exactly what they expected us to pray for, or to whom. But it didn't matter much. We had been praying like hell for the two previous years with singularly little effect.

By February 10 I was back in the hospital compound. I had timed my relapse rather well because quite amazingly I found the food there at the time actually better than outside. We kidded ourselves that this about-face in Nip policy could only mean that they were expecting Allied invasion troops to arrive at any moment and they wanted to be able to show just what humane and considerate little chaps they really were.

Whatever the reason, it was the sick who benefitted from a new dog-trapping campaign launched by the Gunzo. His victims still found themselves slung into the air in Heath Robinson bamboo traps, but he was now beating them to death with his bamboo pole instead of beheading them. And, surprisingly, they were now handed over to the cookhouse specifically for the hospital stew.

Deaths continued to mount slowly. By February 12, 391 bodies

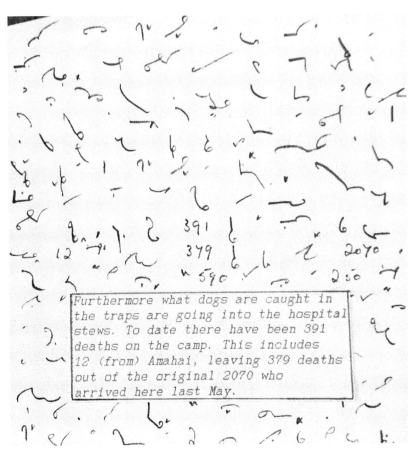

Diary extract from February 12, 1944, ten months after arriving on Haruku

391
379
12
2070
590
250

Furthermore what dogs are caught in the traps are going into the hospital stews. To date there have been 391 deaths on the camp. This includes 12 (from) Amahai, leaving 379 deaths out of the original 2070 who arrived here last May.

had been buried in the makeshift cemetery just outside our barbed wire. We had lost almost a fifth of the camp's original 2075 men.

Thanks perhaps to the dog stew, I made a quick recovery, and within five days had been declared fit enough to join the Gunzo's parties working inside the camp. The Gunzo's treatment of these semi-fit men had earned him the undying hatred of the whole camp, but looking around I had to admit he had brought about some astounding improvements. Only two of the original huts remained. The swamp had vanished, and there were level paths and adequate drainage ditches everywhere. We were certainly in a far better position to face the coming rains than we had been the previous year.

Mind you, the Gunzo had not neglected his own comfort. He had built himself a little bamboo palace, and, oddly enough, sited it on our side of the barbed wire, well away from the rest of the

The Gunzo's nightmare. If Mori was the little king of Haruku, he was a moody, sullen king. Perhaps he foresaw the day when, as in this photo, he himself would be the prisoner. Here he is on the right, without his bamboo pole, without his dark glasses but with Kasi Yama still beside him, after surrendering in Java

Nips. There he lived in splendid isolation, the *de facto* King of Haruku.

Who else but a king could have a round-the-clock armed guard on his favourite fruit tree? The durian tree, surrounded by barbed wire, stood beside the track to the airstrip near the kampong. Its large foul-smelling fruits, renowned as an aphrodisiac, were just beginning to ripen. The Gunzo, perhaps with the brothel in mind, had apparently decided to commandeer them.

Despite his apparently unlimited power, he appeared a lonely man. He lavished what affection he allowed himself to show on a large black cat. His pet certainly fed much better than we did. It did not escape our attention that here was a damned good stew walking around in our midst. And indeed spending a fair amount of time, as it did, around the cookhouse, the animal itself seemed to be courting disaster. But prudence prevailed and we treated the animal with the respect due to the royal favourite. However, its privileged position still proved a mixed blessing. More than one Nip, somewhat battered after an interview with the Gunzo, came stalking the cookhouse on a private "kick the Gunzo's cat" mission. Fortunately for the camp, if not for the whole island, the animal always managed to escape before serious damage was inflicted.

By March 1 I found myself back on outside work as one of a party of 200 removed from the main parade to go to a Nip barracks on the opposite side of the island. We never quite made out who these Nips were. They wore no insignia of rank though each carried a ceremonial sword. The important thing about them was they didn't expect too much of us and didn't get too excited when someone sloped off to look for a fallen coconut or a tapioca root. At the barracks I ended up in a small group under the charge of a particularly young Nip with a smattering of English. Every Nip had to have a name so when he told us he was only 18, he quickly became Ju Achi, which is eighteen in Nipponese.

Ju Achi gave us a stretch of scrub to clear for roadmaking. Finish it, he told us, and you can relax for the rest of the day. As he seemed a fairly harmless sort of chap and the surrounding area looked promising for a little foraging, we took him at his word and got cracking. Before long, right in our path, we came upon a bush containing a hornets' nest. Now in our book you just didn't disturb Haruku hornets, particularly when you were wearing nothing but a tattered pair of shorts. We left them well alone.

So when Ju Achi came along to inspect the finished job he found this bush standing out all alone in the middle of the otherwise cleared track. With the help of a little inspired sign language we explained the reason. A look of utter scorn spread over Ju Achi's youthful features. "You English," he exclaimed in Malay-cum-Nip, "like women. Me Nippon." And, with that, he drew his sword. I didn't actually see the sword strike the hornets' nest. By that time I, along with the rest of the cowardly English, was making a creditable bid on the hundred yard sprint record. We looked back only when we had put sufficient distance between us and the hornets to make clear to them that we had no connection whatever with the impetuous Ju Achi. By that time our young hero was leaping about, and threshing around wildly, inside a cloud of extremely hostile insects. Ju Achi put up a valiant fight in the best Samurai tradition, but, alas, he had very much the worst of the encounter. The battle over, he tried to hide from us the full extent of the damage by superintending our activities from afar. But, even from a distance, it was obvious to us that it was considerable.

Towards evening it began to rain. Rather than join us when we took cover under an atap shelter, he chose to get wet. But the shower developed into a torrential downpour and forced him to come in. He sat at the very edge of the party looking out into the rain. But he could not conceal that there were tears running down his badly-swollen cheeks. We all felt sorry for him, though we couldn't help feeling he had learned a valuable lesson.

We didn't normally waste much sympathy on our captors and when Thomas, who habitually doubted whatever we said or did, had an even more painful lesson, we shed few tears. The Nips, rather surprisingly to us, were very fastidious about baths, and in Haruku baths meant petrol drums, so ridding drums of all traces of their original contents became yet another of our many talents. Thomas set us to work cleaning a few, and when we had finished, accused us of not doing the job properly. Then, to our amazement, he set about examining our work with a lighted taper. We had judiciously moved to a safe distance when an explosion proved that his suspicions about the thoroughness of our work were well founded. We were obviously guilty as charged, but fortunately for us Thomas, lying in a heap on the ground, was in no condition to pass sentence.

Another bright and sunny morning I found myself in a select party of six heading for the interior of the island. Our Nip of the day had such rodent-like features that he became the Rat on sight. He tried to exchange an odd word or two in English, so, in our efforts to encourage this thirst for knowledge, we mentioned his new name. He liked it so much that he kept chuckling "I Ratto" as we trudged along.

The job turned out to involve fencing off an area of bush about half the size of a football pitch. We didn't know quite what for, but nothing mattered except that it was easy work. The fencing comprised anything we could lay our hands on. So some sections, built of coconut logs, would have withstood an elephant charge. But, owing to shortage of material, other parts left something to be desired.

The reason for the exercise became clear during the afternoon when a couple of natives arrived carrying a pig, tied by its feet, on a bamboo pole between them. Not a pink, podgy, English sort of porker, but a scrawny, dark gray specimen with business-like tusks. We assumed that the Nips dreamed of setting up a pig ranch, producing an endless supply of pork chops. An excellent project. We only wished we could do the same ourselves. The wily beast, however had other ideas. It seemed it had quickly sized up the strengths and weaknesses of our stockade because, as soon as it was released into its new home, it shot straight through the fence like a rocket and vanished into the surrounding semi-jungle. A lightning demonstration, in fact, of just how easy it was to escape from a Nip prison. We stood around anxiously, expecting the Rat to vent his rage on us in the usual manner. But he didn't say a word. He marched us back to camp and handed us over to the guards in complete silence. We could only speculate that, having failed his Emperor on what was obviously a vital mission, nothing remained for him but to find a quiet spot to disembowel himself.

Soon Nitty Whiskers, that Nip officer who had given us the reassuring pep talk before we sailed from Java, arrived on the island. He went off arm-in-arm with the Gunzo to some sort of conference on Ambon. According to rumour the problem under discussion appeared to be that the Nips could neither feed us on the island nor get us off, resulting in a cut in our rice ration to 400 grams per man per day.

So preoccupied were we with our food situation that the second anniversary of our surrender passed unnoticed on March 8. Once we had been counting the days: now we forgot the years.

Though the airstrip had become fully operational, we were still sending there working parties. On two successive nights they returned highly delighted to report the crash of a reconnaissance plane. But when a third plane crashed and caught fire alongside a group of prisoners six of them rushed forward to drag out the crew. The Nips responded with a special parade at which the heroes were ceremoniously granted three days off work on treble rations.

In retrospect, it may seem more than a little incongruous that prisoners should save on the ground the lives of men our own side were trying to kill in the air. Perhaps if they had had the time to consider the rights and wrongs of the case in advance, the rescuers might have acted differently. But faced suddenly with the spectacle of men in danger of being incinerated, their spur-of-the-moment reaction had been to get them out of danger. They acted, perhaps, not as friends or foes, but merely as human beings.

Two years earlier there would have been a general outcry that they be court-martialled immediately we were freed. Now freedom and courts-martial seemed as remote as the furthermost stars. Very few of us thought much about the issue. We just envied the rescuers their treble rations.

At long last we observed signs that the Nips had decided to evacuate prisoners from the islands. A Dutch group who had joined us from Amahai were shipped by sampan to Ambon to await, they learned, a ship for Java. Another 400 men were chosen to move out as soon as possible.

The reduction in numbers did nothing to increase our rations. On the contrary, the situation became so bad that the Nips announced on working parade permission for us to scrounge anything edible we could lay our hands on. Relieved of the need to smuggle all loot past the guards on return to camp, and with parties now road-building all over the island, we carried out the order with tremendous enthusiasm. Graduating from the usual leaves, I experimented with such wild delicacies as blimbing bulu, small cucumber-shaped berries that tasted vaguely like gooseberries, loobiloobies, tiny bitter cherries; and fool's curry, a root which gave the rice a yellowish tinge, if it failed to do much for the flavour. Needless to say there were some accidents. I discovered that the underskin of old tapioca roots is highly poisonous by making myself violently sick. Unidentified roots and fruits were always risky, but none, so far as I know, proved fatal.

Then came the afternoon when one of my wildest dreams came true, well almost. I was standing in a steam, collecting boulders for road-making, when I noticed something feathery floating towards me. I lurched across to pull from the water... a whole chicken. I was absolutely intoxicated with this astounding stroke of good fortune. At long last the fates were treating me as I deserved.

It was only with extreme difficulty that the rest of the party, who had quickly gathered round to see this amazing find, persuaded me that the bright green hue of the flesh meant not only that the bird was not exactly fresh, but must have been positively lethal. With great reluctance I let my greatest prize as a Pow fall back into the stream.

April 29, and a gift from the Emperor himself on the occasion of the royal birthday. To our astonishment each of us was presented with a 2ft. 6in. square of flower-patterned blue cloth. How a thousand-odd cotton squares came to arrive in God-forsaken, starving Haruku must rank as one of the great mysteries of WWII. What they were supposed to be used for we never discovered. Presumably the Nips had asked themselves the same question, and then some genius had suggested giving them to us.

However, this was the first sign of such generosity since the Jaarmarkt boots, so some sort of action was called for. I desperately needed some shorts. Perhaps this scarf, or handkerchief, or whatever it was, could be converted into a pair.

There were difficulties. So far as I knew only one needle existed in the hut, and it was suddenly in great demand: I put myself down on the waiting list. There was no cotton at all, but I kept my diary in a rough canvas holder, and I found that, with a little patience, I could tease out strands of cotton from the canvas. Elastic to hold the things up? I managed to scrounge an old pair of bootlaces to use instead. The biggest problem of all was how to go about actually making the wretched things. To start with, I hadn't the slightest idea, but during my long wait for the needle it eventually dawned on me that all I had to do was use an existing pair of shorts as a template; lay them on the floor and cut round them twice. And in due course I succeeded in converting a useless piece of cloth into what I considered an elegant item of menswear.

I was not the only one to show quite unexpected talent with the needle, and not the only one to appear on working parade with a large flower convering my backside. It did arouse a certain amount of comment, but leaders of fashion can always expect a certain amount of ignorant abuse.

On May 3 and 4, 250 of the sick left unhappily for Ambon. Unhappily, because when they were crammed into sampans for the short sea crossing they were forced to abandon their pathetic little bundles of luggage. So they set out into the unknown without the precious tin cans they were always hoping to have something to cook in, without the lice-infested blankets that could make life just a little more endurable on a chilly night or torrential rain, without the few possessions which marked them out as human beings rather than a shipload of cattle.

Back on the airstrip, listening to the jabbering of the Nips during air-raid alarms, it became clear that they were facing a new menace, what they called the san ju achi. This was the American P38 fighter, which put fear into their hearts and new hope into ours. We reckoned that if this twin-boom Lockheed Lightning could be escort bombers over the islands, the Allied bases must be close by.

On our jobs away from the airstrip we saw more of the islanders. Some, we gathered, were Christians sympathetic towards the Allies. Others were Muslims, co-operating enthusiastically with the Nips. The camp shop was a sort of United Nations operation, supplies for the British and Dutch prisoners being obtained by the Nips from Christian traders through a Muslim intermediary.

After one delivery the go-between apparently thought he could exploit the complexities of the situation. Confident that the traders would be too frightened to protest, he pocketed their money and told them the Nips had refused to pay. Sure enough the traders decided they would be on a beating to nothing if they dared to accuse the Nips of cheating them. They said nothing but, anxious not to be robbed a second time, they stopped coming. The Nips regarded this as an insult, and began making inquiries. The truth came out, and the pro-Nip Muslim found that the Nips were quite impartial when it came to handing out their particular brand of justice. For some reason, perhaps to intimidate us, they chose one of our huts as the torture-chamber.

After savage beatings, the go-between was suspended upside down while boiling water was poured over him. Next he was made to kneel by a cooking fire while Nips burned him about the body with glowing coconut husks. The Gunzo rounded off the session by urinating over him. He was then taken away, presumably to be executed. Another native, who had been selling us tobacco in quiet corners out on working parties, was brought into camp accused of having stolen the tobacco. He, too, tasted Nip justice.

These punishments, with the victims' cries echoing round our huts, resulted in a tense atmosphere, reminding us of the sort of people our captors could be. We pitied the tortured, no matter what they had done, and dreaded that next time it could be one of us.

Meanwhile the Gunzo decided that the whole camp needed a little punishment. So each morning before work, and each evening after work, he had everyone in the camp running about carrying boulders nowhere in particular.

He offered no reason, but we had our own ideas. One was that the current rumour, that the Nips had just lost three battleships and an aircraft carrier, was true, and we were doing penance for the sins of the Americans. The other theory was that the Gunzo had put all his ill-gotten Haruku gains, such as watches and rings, on a ship bound for home and had just heard that all were now at the bottom of the Banda Sea.

The thought that either possibility might be true considerably lightened the weight of the boulders, and, anyway, as it imposed heavy strains on the guards themselves to make sure every man was carrying one, this punishment seemed to be forgotten after a few days, and we resumed our normal treadmill day, which itself kept us in perpetual motion from our morning pap to the lights-out bugle, when we finally flopped exhausted on to the bamboo.

13: MOMENT OF TRUTH

June – July, 1944.   Haruku, South Moluccas

With fewer men now hopping in and out of the hospital area, the constant reshuffling of our places on the bamboo began to abate. Life in the huts became more stable, and little groups began to form to make life a little easier by sharing chores and resources. In fact the Navy lads formed themselves into one big coconut commando, and the Welsh, too, had a sizeable mafia. I settled for a small exclusive co-operative with Sid, my partner in the encounter with the Mad Monk, and another neighbour who had been with me in Semarang.

Our first joint success was the killing of a couple of snakes which had had the misfortune to set up home in a heap of stones the Nips wanted us to move elsewhere. We bore our prizes, rather thinner than we would have liked but each about 3 ft long, back to camp in triumph. Preparing them for the pot proved no trouble at all. Once we'd removed the heads, the skins peeled away almost like taking off a stocking. The innards came away cleanly from the flesh and in no time we had snake cutlets. Luckily I had just smuggled some coconut oil into camp in my RAF waterbottle, a very useful piece of equipment. So, it was fried snake for supper. Sadly it was rather like chewing indiarubber, though we all said what a wonderful meal it made, and felt sure of deriving some benefit from this obviously rich protein.

Shortly afterwards Sid brought off our biggest coup. Though the last native tobacco baron had come to a violent end, it was not long before a successor appeared. Sid managed to contact him, buy a thick wad at a very reasonable price, and convey it safely back into camp. We cut it up into small quantities and sold it at a quite exorbitant profit. Even now some nicotine addicts seemed to prefer a smoke to a meal.

After Sid's example I felt I should make a worthwhile contribution to our little combine. I thought my big chance had come when I found myself on a small working party heading for a new part of the island. The coconut palms and canaris trees lining our track gave way to a small kampong. And it seemed to be market day. Our eyes popped out at the sight of stalls laden with sliced papayas, pineapples, sun-dried fish and tapioca biscuits. We'd seen nothing like it throughout our term of imprisonment. If only I could get in there! That, of course, was out of the question. But our Nip (we had christened him Dopey) didn't seem too unfriendly, and obviously didn't know the rules. Could I just possibly persuade him to do a little shopping for me on the way back?

As the day dragged on, I managed to strike up a Nip-cum-Malay conversation with him. He showed some interest in the Middle East, so I gave him a detailed lecture, illustrated with drawings in the dust, of my exploits as a rear-gunner on a camel in the Western Desert. He seemed very impressed. So, on the way back to camp, I put the big question to him. Would he buy me some dried fish at the kampong?

He made no reply, and I wrote off the enterprise as a waste of time. But then, as we came up to the kampong, he called a halt-and motioned me to go into the market. For a moment, I just couldn't believe it. The slightest communication with the islanders was a near capital, if indeed not capital, offence, yet here was a Nip so ignorant of the rules that he was inviting me to go in among them. Still I couldn't back out now. So, bringing out the cash I kept hidden for just such an emergency, I hurried off.

At my approach the market jabbering stopped abruptly. Shoppers backed away as though I had cholera. When I reached the dried fish the stallholder cowered behind his wares with terror in his eyes, muttering something about Nippon. "Nippon knows, Nippon knows," I assured him in Malay.

Then a grunted "Koorah" drew my attention to a swarthy Nip waddling towards me under his oversize dome-shaped topee. A fist caught me across the side of the face and, almost simultaneously it seemed, a foot dug in to my guts. For once I was glad to see a familiar Nip, Dopey, hurrying across to see what the commotion was about. There was a long staccato burst of Nip from beneath the topee. Dopey muttered confusedly and ordered me back to join his party. I marched back to camp emptyhanded but still in one piece.

That, I hoped, was the end of the matter. But next morning Dopey came stalking along the working parade to single me out to join his party. I soon found out why. All day he kept me staggering up a slippery riverbank through some particularly thorny sago palms, carrying the heaviest boulders he could find, and encouraging me with well-aimed kicks and blows whenever I showed signs of flagging. Whether this was just the result of the market confrontation or whether he had been discussing camel rear-gunners with less gullible mates I could only conjecture.

I was not the only one victimised that day for showing a little enterprise. When I limped wearily back into camp I passed two friends standing tied to trees by the entrance, each with a fish sticking out of his mouth. It would have been suicide to approach them, but I discovered later that the Nips had been out fishing with hand grenades. They had sent a few prisoners, my two friends included, into the sea to bring in the catch they had blasted to the surface. Quite naturally, my friends felt they deserved some reward for their efforts, and each had been caught with a fish hidden in his shorts.

June began with 48 hours' incessant downpour which turned the gardens back into swamp, and high winds which brought coconut trees crashing down around the camp. Despite the storm, bombers continued to drone over the island. Nips seemed to be leaving in little groups by sampan. There was a definite end-of-term atmosphere.

Then, surprisingly, as though they thought everything was coming up roses, the Nips produced postcards and a selection of wish-you-were-here sentences for us to choose from for our first messages home from Haruku. Why we got the cards at this time was a mystery. Perhaps some Nip came across them while clearing out his stationery cupboard before leaving for Java. We couldn't believe they would ever reach Britain, but we wrote them just in case. Mine certainly never made it.

There was talk of an invasion of France. We dismissed D-day as just another rumour.

Work continued in its usual crazy way. For some time I managed to avoid the airstrip. When I did return, along with Sid, something new had been added. Beside the atap shelter the Nips used as an office-cum-toolshed, a wire-netting cage had been erected. In it, pecking optimistically at the coral, were half a dozen scrawny hens. And in a corner hung a nestbox.

During the long months on Haruku, whenever I'd dreamt of food, which was often, I'd dreamt of eggs. All that morning, as I went through the pretence of hacking at coral with my chunkel, I was weighing up the chances of there being such treasure in the nestbox. And the more I thought about them the more I craved for them.

It was something more than coincidence that I was outside the henhouse on my way back from the latrines when an air-raid warning sounded. I'd been hanging about that wirenetting in spirit all morning. I looked carefully around me. The only people, prisoners or Nips, that I could see were racing to put as much distance as possible between themselves and the runway.

Without daring to think of the possible consequences, I unfastened the henhouse door and leapt across to the nestbox. I felt the wonderful smooth shape of five eggs. I grabbed them. Then I checked myself, and reluctantly put three back. Perhaps two might not be missed. Five certainly would. I dashed out of the enclosure closing the door carefully behind me.

Fearfully I looked around again, half expecting to find an angry Nip bearing down on me with bayonet fixed. But there was not a soul anywhere near. I ran off, holding the precious eggs in a pocket of the old Dutch army tunic I had put on that morning to keep out the rain. As quickly as I could, I caught up with the stragglers in the air-raid stampede.

No bombers materialised out of the dreary storm-black sky, the all-clear sounded, and we slouched back to work. It was a tense, nervy sort of day. The Nips, unsettled by the continuing air raids, turned more bad-tempered and edgy than usual. I comforted myself by fondling the treasures in my pocket.

At long last the joyous sound of the knocking-off bugle echoed over the coral hills. The various gangs began to assemble for the inevitable tenko check before heading back to camp.

By the time our party joined them a buzz was going round the ranks that two men were being held by the Nips on the far side of the airstrip. They had been beaten up for wandering off to look for coconuts during the air-raid alert and were now tied to trees. I wondered how my crime compared to theirs. The eggs in my pocket began to feel a little hot to my touch.

Then came another buzz: the Nips were looking for someone

who had robbed their henhouse. Now the eggs were burning a hole in my pocket. I looked anxiously around me. Perhaps I could stamp the eggs into the ground. But there were Nips everywhere.

Once we were all herded into ranks, a dapper little Nip stepped forward to address the parade. "Today," he said in Malay, "hens very much work. Before air raid alert five eggs. But after air raid alert only three eggs." Then came the announcement I was dreading. Every man was to be searched. Sid immediately offered to take the eggs from me. I was almost coward enough to let him. But not quite. I shivered with fear as the great egg hunt got under way. We stood as usual in double file. Two Nips, one tackling each row, worked their way towards us. Carefully they examined haversacks and hats. Roughly they frisked bodies. After being searched, each man had to move some 20 paces to the right to join those cleared for the march back to camp.

"They're just wasting everybody's time," grumbled someone behind me. "Anyone with any sense would have had those eggs in his belly, raw, hours ago."

I wished to God I had had that sense. Just what could I possible do with the wretched things now? Apart from my jacket all I was wearing was my coolie hat and my home-made shorts. And they didn't even have a pocket. But I did have one spare pocket, torn from an old jacket and carried around as a receptacle for any cigarette ends Nips might chance to drop.

This gave me an idea. Not much of an idea, but the only chance I had. Quickly I dropped the eggs into it, tied it on to the end of the bootlace "elastic" holding up my shorts and let it dangle down inside my shorts between my legs. Fearfully I awaited the searchers. All too soon my Nip arrived. He looked into my hat, examined the contents of my haversack and felt my jacket pockets. He hesitated. I held my breath. Then he moved on to search Sid. I was 20 paces from safety.

It was the longest 20 paces I've ever covered... 20 paces when I was alone and exposed between the ranks of the searched and unsearched, and under the scrutiny of the various Nips standing around watching the proceedings. Walking with two eggs between my legs was a problem it itself, and I really hadn't had the time to ensure that I had tied my knot securely. I waddled along fearing with every step that the eggs would be crushed between my thighs leaving tell-tale streams of yolk running down my legs,

Part of the diary which Don Peacock kept during the whole of his imprisonment. During searches he put it in a prominent position to make sure it was ignored. The edges of the bag he kept it in are tattered where he unthreaded the canvas for sewing cotton

or that the pocket would come loose from the bootlace, depositing the eggs on the deck at my feet.

But I made it. And safe among the innocents, with the Nips' attentions concentrated on those still being searched, I fished the eggs out from their hiding place and put them back in my jacket pocket.

There was another moment or two of anxiety when we arrived back at camp. I braced myself for another search, but, perhaps because we were so late, we were quickly dismissed. Seconds later I was home and dry in my hut. I thanked all the gods I could think of, and, in that moment of truth, decided that I was definitely not of the stuff that heroes are made. That night Sid and I fried the eggs in coconut oil and placed them reverently on top of the evening rice. It was not so much a meal, more the realisation of the wildest of dreams.

We felt like kings, until we found that a couple of blokes in our hut were sharing nothing less than a tin of meat. They had acquired this fantastic luxury, they said, from the Navy lads in the next hut in exchange for two miraculously well-preserved shirts and a blanket. And the Navy didn't sell only one tin of meat. It soon became clear that they were in business in a big way. Within a few weeks they seemed to have bought most of the best clothes and bedding in the camp, to say nothing of the odd wristwatch. And they fed like fighting cocks into the bargain.

Naturally their success aroused a certain amount of envy, not to say plain bloody jealousy. Just about everybody in the camp was keen to get in on the act. That is until it became general knowledge that the path to riches lay through a hole in the back of a foodstore at a Nip barracks.

It was a path few cared to tread, except an RAF corporal called Dennis. He shadowed the Navy, discovered exactly how and where they worked their miracle, and decided that what they could do, so could he. He, too, went through the hole at the back of the foodstore, only to be grabbed by a native guard. The Nips had apparently discovered the discrepancies and laid their trap. Dennis, who had stolen absolutely nothing out of the store, walked right into it. His capture plunged the camp into fearful gloom. The Nips would not regard this as the usual petty smuggling or pilfering, but as serious crime.

The whole camp was ordered out on to the large dusty parade ground. Two guards dragged Dennis out of a hut at the side and frogmarched him across to the centre of the stage where the Gunzo awaited his victim. We stood there, helpless, forced to witness yet another agonising spectacle of Nip brutality.

Yet it was with something akin to relief that we watched the Gunzo begin lashing out with his bamboo pole. We had feared that Dennis might be shot, or even beheaded. A merciless beating of a mild, slightly-built chap followed, but, like all prisoners I knew who suffered this treatment, Dennis showed astonishing guts, standing his ground as long as he could, and then, when he was eventually felled, striving blindly back up on to his feet. At length he was, mercifully, knocked out completely, then dragged away to a Nip cell to await the next session.

Perhaps it seems crazy that Dennis, and so many others like him, stood up as long as humanly possible under such savage punishment. On the face of it this appeared quite a senseless gesture of defiance. But, whatever the truth of it, it seemed to impress the Nips, and it could be that their respect for courage often deterred them from handing out to prisoners the horrific torture they so frequently inflicted on the natives. Dennis's beatings went on for several days. How many I didn't record. I was afraid to write about it in case my diary ever came into the hands of a Nip who could read it. But, at long last, the Gunzo sent Dennis his ritual bunch of bananas, to show that all was forgiven and there was, in any case, nothing personal about this frenzied brutality. Dennis, sadly, never completely recovered, and died a few weeks later on a boat on the way back to Java.

July brought a new batch of rumours of Nip defeats. Their much vaunted 'Greater East Asia' was said to be crumbling all around them. All we knew for certain was that American bombers flew busily over the islands day and night, hammering Nip shipping. So it was with very mixed feelings that 250 of us, euphemis-

Once the scene here was reminiscent of the building of the Pyramids with hundreds of Pow slaves toiling under the Nip lash to provide an advance base for Hirohito's warplanes. But Dave Harries found that although Haruku now has electricity and a road the bush has reclaimed the airfield

137

tically described as "the less fit," greeted the order on the night of July 12 to be ready to sail from Haruku the next day. The hated island suddenly became almost attractive, for the Yanks were coming and their battle for the island would no doubt prove a sticky period. The Nips might well shoot us all as soon as any invasion began, but we had to face this danger somewhere sometime, perhaps the sooner the better.

However our feelings were purely academic. Certainly no one was going to consult us about our future. And early next morning, the thirteenth, we were packed into sampans to sail to Ambon, en route, we were told, for Java. It was lucky thirteen in at least one respect; heavy rain with low cloud protected us from the danger of air attack. Sid was not with us. He was designated one of the "more fit." Sadly I never saw him again.

Haruku had been an island of misery, starvation, disease and death, but I have one favourite memory. It is of a blazing hot morning when a group of jet black, pro-Allies Ambonese arrived on the airstrip to strengthen the coolie labour force. The Nips kept us well apart, but the new arrivals soon found a way of expressing their sympathy. Across the sizzling coral, cool and clear, came the sound of a hundred voices singing that wonderful Christmas carol "Silent Night." They sang in Dutch, but the message couldn't have been clearer.

14: "WAVE TO THE BOMBERS"

July – September, 1944. Ambon, Celebes, Java.

My most vivid recollection of Liang, first stop on the long road back from Haruku, is of a camp of hollow-eyed, emaciated caricatures of men sitting on their haunches in the shadow of their huts, staring at the bare earth as though waiting for some remotely edible weed to push its way to the surface. All traces of vegetation within the barbed wire boundaries had long since disappeared into the cooking pots.

The camp on the south coast of Ambon Island was the place where, some months earlier, the working party from Haruku had reported that there had once been chicken on the black market. It had certainly gone down the ratings in the prisoners' *Good Food Guide* by the time we arrived.

True the daily rice ration, which we were told had been as low as 325 grams, against 400 in Haruku, had been jacked up to 600, about 21 oz, just before our arrival, but there was practically nothing to go with it.

Each day Nip guards took out a party of prisoners to scour the surrounding hills for any sort of edible green matter. They generally came back with a sack or two of green weeds, but these didn't do a great deal to put flesh on the bones of the camp's 1500 inmates.

Neither could there be any possibility of private-enterprise foraging. Just 300 men a day were sent out to work, and then only as far as the adjacent airstrip. There was nothing to pinch there, or on the short march to it. On Haruku, no matter how grim the present, there had always been the hope of bringing home the bacon, or at any rate a tapioca root or two, on some brighter tomorrow. In Liang there seemed no tomorrow, just a dreary repetition of a despairing today.

Of course, although there seemed to be no possible way of smuggling any goodies in, the camp still had its black market, fed presumably by corruption in high places. But the sort of money we had brought from Haruku proved useless. The acute shortage of supplies had fired hyper-inflation, and prices rose to the astronomical. A coconut cost two and a half dollars, 25 times a day's pay, while a spoonful of salt set you back a dollar. We just could not compete.

So far as it was run at all, the camp was still a British Army show. We saw very little of the Nips, and we actually missed the little bastards. Even at the worst of times dodging and, hopefully, outwitting them, added a little sparkle to life. Their eccentricities provided a frequent source of amusement. On its day the Nip Army Game amused us as much as an ENSA show. Without them, we dragged out the days discussing rumours no-one believed and waiting to hear who had died. As Liang still treated its dead to The Last Post, the bugle echoed mournfully around the surrounding hills every day. Up to our arrival thirteen Haruku men had ended their journey back to Java in the makeshift cemetery here, and it was soon evident that if we stayed very long many more would join them.

Our prospects were not enhanced by the weather. Days of torrential rain proved too much for the atap roofs. Every bit of clothing became damp and clammy, if not actually soaked. Everyone was cold and miserable. And the wettest and most miserable of all were the small group of men who kept arriving from Haruku, looking as if they had swum over. They told us that it seemed that all remaining prisoners were being evacuated from the heavily-bombed island.

It was still raining on August 16 when 600 men moved out of Liang for Ambon town and, they hoped, an early boat to Java. The sick, many desperately ill, lay out in the downpour on the backs of open lorries. But they welcomed any way of getting out of the wretched place.

As soon as the rains eased the bombers returned, attacking the uncomfortably close airstrip. Already one Dutchman had been killed inside the camp when bombs overshot their target. We looked on as 21 black evil-looking bombers, escorted by 12 quicksilver P38s, plastered the runway where we had men working. One was killed and eight others seriously injured. But this time the bombers did destroy eight Nips as well. Obviously working parties were not very popular, and, equally obviously, before long

I found myself picked out for one. The scene that met us when we struggled on to the airstrip did nothing to abate my forebodings, for the place had been reduced to an aircraft graveyard. The planes that remained were so peppered with holes that they looked more like gigantic nutmeg-graters.

Our job consisted of walking in long lines up and down the runway picking up the jagged pieces of shrapnel which threatened the tyres of any plane taking off or landing. The Nips behaved half-heartedly about the work: they must have realised, as well as we did, that we were all wasting our time, for no planes would take off, and probably none would land either. When we were midway down the landing strip, the air-raid alarm sounded. We looked around uneasily, wondering if we could take shelter. But we needn't have worried about the Nips. Lorries came sweeping in to pick them up. They clambered hurriedly aboard and sped off, leaving us to our own devices. A frantic search located a couple of roofed shelters. We piled into them. And, as we lay there in a heap, the whole area was sprayed with those rather unsporting anti-personnel bombs.

As it would have been asking to be decapitated to look out of our trenches, we never exactly identified the raiders. But we would have loved to point out to them that the only personnel around were prisoners already half dead anyway, the only planes were wrecks and the only result of the operation was that we had a damned sight more shrapnel to pick up when the Nips eventually decided it was safe to return.

When we staggered wearily back to camp we found nothing but confusion. It appeared the local Nips had no more idea than we had of what was going on around us. Ambon was becoming a Singapore in reverse. Every plane was a Yank, and the Nips had absolutely no answer to them. Fortunately some guardian angel somewhere decided to get us out of Liang. Men began leaving in small daily batches. We felt they could not be joining a boat because the numbers were too small, but that any change must be an improvement. I hadn't long to wait before I could judge for myself. On August 14 I formed part of a lorry-load of prisoners dumped outside a tangle of barbed wire high on the outskirts of Ambon town.

Inside the wire a school, a church and a house had been combined to form a makeshift transit camp, already grossly overcrowded. Confined indoors by a bunch of jittery armed guards, we found it difficult to get our bearings accurately, but the town seemed to spill down from our hill to the huge landlocked bay which made Ambon such an excellent naval base. We had the luxury of a sound roof over our heads for the first time in two years, but we would have preferred something to eat, having to exist on two plates of pap a day.

We waited five days in this hell-hole, expecting at any moment to be moved down the hill and on to the Java boat. On the sixth a group of guards called to collect us, herding us down through the streets of the town to the shore. The whole place seemed deserted, but by a jetty some sampans were moored.

We were hustled aboard, and the sampans chugged quickly out into the bay. Away ahead of us, widely dispersed, no doubt to present as difficult a target as possible, a few small cargo boats lay at anchor. Some of my shipmates began making bets as to which would be ours. We approached near enough to one ship to start worrying about her rusting decks and peeling paintwork, but just as we had decided that she was ours, we changed course. Soon it became evident that there was no ship for us and we were heading straight out across the bay, and it was there that we eventually tied up at a small jetty.

We stumbled ashore through coconut palms to a scene of unbelievable desolation where a derelict camp's wrecked huts still housed a few native labourers, in a pitiable plight. Many looked desperately ill, but they seemed to get no help from anyone. Four or five died each day. The survivors had not the strength to bury the dead properly. The graves in the cemetery behind the camp had been dug so shallow that the whole area stank of rotting flesh. Hundreds of coolies were said to have died here at Tiga Rumah. There could have been an epidemic of cholera perhaps, or maybe the Nips had just worked them till they dropped, and then abandoned them.

A party of prisoners who had arrived a week or two before us had cleaned up available parts of the camp that could be made habitable. But with our arrival, swelling the numbers to 1,600, there was nothing like enough space to go round. We latecomers had to build whatever shelter we could out of the débris or just sleep in the open. Mercifully the rains had eased off.

Food proved to be practically non-existent. The earlier arrivals had been sent to work on the ships in the bay and existed mainly on what they had been able to steal from them. Of course they were searched each time they came ashore, but the Tiga Rumah Nips, who were getting very little food themselves, had no intention of punishing anyone. They took a share of the loot and encouraged the prisoners to bring more next time.

Air raids were just part of the daily routine. American planes cruised low overhead with complete impunity. There was no fighter resistance whatsoever, and ack-ack fire was sporadic. And this was just the warm-up. Noon on August 28 saw the start of the Ambon blitz.

I was walking through the camp, minding my own business, when, totally without warning, a flight of P38s came skimming over the palm tops, blasting away with cannon. In one fantastic leap I was at the bottom of a latrine, fortunately newly dug and unused. As I landed, I felt an excruciating pain in my right ankle. Simultaneously some half dozen chaps fell on top of me. I swore in

The Lockheed Lightning P38 (San-ju-achi to the Nips) which escorted the bombers raiding Ambon. It was also responsible for Don Peacock's sprained ankle, sustained when he leapt into a latrine to avoid its cannon fire. (Imperial War Museum)

143

protest, but had to remain pinned down in agony until the men on top had decided the danger had passed. I crawled out in time to see the Lightnings blast away at some target, real or imagined, farther along the shore, and then bank to go swooping low over the sea to strafe the cargo ships. I tried to stand, but the pain from my ankle was unbearable. So I lay by my funkhole watching, fascinated, as the bomber force followed up the fighters. They came in from the east in tight little groups of three. I began counting them, but gave up at 76. Not many perhaps when compared with the armadas which were at that time attacking German cities, but a colossal number to be launched against the corrugated tin and atap shacks on the other side of the bay.

It rained incendiaries and anti-personnel bombs, interspersed with the occasional big one. The town area appeared to have become one gigantic inferno. I felt a sudden chill as a huge pall of smoke rose to blot out the sun. I thought fearfully of the two small parties of prisoners who had sailed across the bay that morning with high hopes of a day's foraging as they worked in the town. I heard later that they had got clear of the main target area during the initial strafing, but two had been killed outright and many others badly hurt.

Those who came back said the Nips had suffered very heavy casualties, but that, as usual, the worst sufferers had been the native population. They believed, too, that many Aussies had been killed at a camp near the naval dockyard somewhere round the bay.

Amid all this death and destruction one prisoner's injured ankle may seem rather trivial, but it felt of surpeme importance to me: if ever there had been a time in my life when I needed all my wits and all my limbs, this was it.

My cares were not exactly swept away when I found a doctor. After a cursory glance at my foot, by now ominously swollen, he explained cheerfully that there was just no way in which he could find out whether the ankle was broken or just badly strained, and very little he could do about it either way. He gave me a bandage and the best prescription he could offer: "Hope for the best."

Everyone else was busy digging for survival. No trench could be deep enough. I wished I could join them. Some sort of action, any sort of action, was better than just lying there wondering what would happen next.

A few new arrivals kept trickling into camp from Haruku and Liang. All had their own stories of heavy strafing and bombing. The Yanks were coming. And this time it was no rumour. Again we wondered if we'd be better off staying put, facing starvation, more bombing and an extremely doubtful future when the invasion began, or sailing out to face the very real danger of ending up feeding the sharks in the Banda Sea: useless speculation, because our fate had been taken completely out of our hands.

For five hundred of us the die was cast on August 31, when the Nips ordered us aboard two of the ships in the bay. For a while I thought I would miss the boat because I was physically incapable of making my way to the shore. But friends found a sack-and-bamboo stretcher no longer needed by its last occupant. Four of them carried me shoulder-high down to the waiting sampans.

Two hundred of us were put aboard a motorship, small, modern and, I hoped, fast and manoeuvrable. We stretcher-cases were lowered into the hold first, and balanced ourselves on top of the cargo: hundreds of empty petrol barrels. An explosion risk, I thought, but it was comforting to have a life-raft handy.

There was no hanging about. The skipper was more than anxious to be off. We sailed with the guards still trying to push the last of the party down into the hold. But the Nips had no sooner got everyone below decks than they started urging everyone up again. There were planes coming in low, and they wanted us to wave, display any bit of British uniform we possessed, do anything to persuade the aircrews to leave the ship alone. Whether the raiders saw us, or cared much anyway, I don't know, but we sailed out of the bay unscathed. However we hadn't quite seen the last of Ambon. While the skipper couldn't get out of the bay quick enough, he apparently wasn't too keen on the open sea either, at least not in daylight. We nosed close to shore in a little cove and dropped anchor to await the cover of darkness. The men on deck were driven back down below.

We sailed as darkness fell. The atmosphere was tense down in the crowded hold on that first night at sea. With a little manoeuvring of the petrol drums I contrived to get my stretcher balanced for maximum comfort. The sea felt calm and ship's-roll barely perceptible, the engines being smooth and remarkably quiet. But still sleep did not come easily.

I lay awake straining my ears for the sound I least wanted to hear... the drone of planes. As I had proved repeatedly I was no hero in air raids on land, but I feared them much more at sea, particularly after that morning of terror on the *Empire Star*, a lifetime ago, before I was conscripted into the Nip army.

As on the *Cho Saki Maru*, which had brought us out from Java, just one set of rungs led out of the hold. I eyed them unhappily, and tried to banish thoughts of being trapped below decks as the ship went down, or of floating precariously on a petrol barrel surrounded by a blazing sea.

I was not the only man scared to death that night. In fact the only prisoners who were not worried were those beyond it, the desperately ill on the stretchers around me. One of them, a Dutchman, passed away during the night from injuries received in the Ambon blitz.

The other stretcher-cases were, for the most part, suffering in various ways from the same basic complaint: starvation. Those dying now were generally of two types, the big and strong or those who had had comparatively privileged jobs, in the cook-house for instance, while we were in Haruku. The heftier men were just not getting enough nourishment to keep their bodies functioning any longer. The cookhouse types could not face the sudden drop to the meagre rations to which the rest of us had become accustomed more gradually.

A couple of stretchers away from me was the man who had once been my CO in Singapore, a man built like a front-row rugger forward and with the looks of a film star, now reduced to a helpless bundle of skin and bone.

Sheer exhaustion eventually overcame the fear and misery of our situation, and most of us fell asleep. Next morning some of the fit climbed up the ladder out on to the deck. The Nips made no attempt to stop them. Perhaps they felt they would need someone to wave at the bombers again if we were attacked. I longed to get away from the horror around me on the stretchers in the hold. And although my ankle was extremely painful, I managed to crawl across to the rungs and drag myself up on deck. It was a beautiful morning. Not a cloud in the sky. Three ships were ploughing through an empty blue sea: ours, another carrying the three hundred men who left Tiga Rumah with us; and a rather diminutive gunboat.

We no longer suffered harassment from the Nips. It seemed as if, temporarily at least, our rôles had changed slightly. We were no longer blustering conquerors and submissive conquered, but all very expendable pawns in the lunatic game of war, wondering if terror, if not death itself, might be lurking just over the horizon.

By mid-morning a bucket of pap arrived on deck. It looked more suitable for wall-papering than eating, but we wolfed it down hungrily. The day wore on with never a plane or ship to disturb our peace of mind, the only excitement being the sharing-out of a second bucket of pap in the evening. Twenty-four hours of peace restored our calm, or some of it, and when darkness brought its added protection, we lay our heads down with just a little more confidence.

Dawn next day found our little convoy sailing along a narrow channel with low, barren-looking land to the north and what appeared to be a wooded coral cliff to the south. Our barrack-room navigators calculated, or at any rate guessed, that we had safely crossed the Banda Sea and had reached the south-east leg of the starfish-shaped island of Celebes.

About 1 p.m. we swung in towards the land to the north, and shortly afterwards tied up alongside a small jetty. We seemed to have arrived at Port Nowhere, with two or three houses among some low scrub, a half-hearted attempt at some sort of cultivation, and a backcloth of low treeless hills. And, so far as we could see, no sign of life whatsoever. It was at this godforsaken corner of the globe that my old CO was buried, along with another British prisoner. The Dutchman had been quietly slid over the ship's side earlier. The burial party had scarcely embarked when the engines sprang into life, and started to move again after a stop of no more than three hours. But we sailed only a mile or two, then crept close in to land, as if to be as inconspicuous as possible, and dropped anchor. The second prison ship joined us, but the gunboat vanished.

The next day being September 3, I calculated that Britain had been at war five years, and we had spent two and a half of them working for the wrong side. However we did no harm to the Allied cause that day or the next. Our ship remained at anchor. We lay wearily on deck, ate our pap, and hoped for the best.

That second night we awoke to the sound of low-flying planes. Bombs came crashing down nearby, but mercifully the raiders failed to find our ships. We experienced another moment of anxi-

147

ety next morning when a dive-bomber came plummeting down at us, but as its bomb doors opened and a black object came dropping towards us, we saw the fried egg on its side. It was one of theirs. The black object turned out to be a harmless canister. It fell into the sea near the ship, and a couple of sailors lowered a dinghy to retrieve it, thinking that it carried orders. We hoped it said "Get cracking" as we were anxious to be on the move towards some grub. We were unlucky. The ship remained obstinately at anchor.

But the fact that we couldn't move towards food didn't mean that food couldn't move towards us. And a little way along the lonely coast the gods, disguised as natives, were preparing a minor miracle. Our first inkling of the wonders in store was the sight of a couple of bumboats paddling towards our ship. They slowed down as they drew nearer, then hung about at a safe distance. They were near enough for us to see that they were loaded with fruit, and we simply willed them to come closer. At last they began to paddle cautiously in, and, getting no hostile reaction from the Nips, eventually drew alongside.

The natives were still uncertain, but the Nips were hungry and ready to do business. Soon little baskets of food were swinging up on to the deck. Seeing the Nips stuffing themselves didn't do much to fill our empty bellies, but we now had the sort of food we had only been able to dream about almost within touching distance. We just had to try for it even if it did mean risking bringing the Nips wading in amongst us lashing out with their rifle butts.

We began calling to the traders and waving our money. There was no reaction from the guards, but, unfortunately, none from the natives either. They were too scared of the Nips to even look at us. However we had to get something now. We kept yelling, and at last, as trade with the Nips began to slacken off, one native, a little bolder than the rest, chanced his neck. He paddled along to our part of the deck and made the first deal with an eager prisoner. We waited for the storm to break. Nothing happened. Then Nips appeared to be turning a blind eye. More bumboats had arrived by this time all ready for business. Soon we were all hauling up baskets of oranges, bananas, sun-dried fish and even eggs. As well as these private deals, we were able to do a bit of collective buying too. And that night we finished off an afternoon of feasting with the richest soup east of Java and, most fantastic of all, an individual piece of fried chicken apiece.

That night we were at peace with the world, even with the Nips, who had not only allowed us to trade, but had also provided cooking facilities for our collective purchases. Perhaps it would not be exaggerating to say we went to sleep happy, for happiness is to a large extent a comparative state of mind, and after Haruku and Ambon, this remote backwater, which the traders referred to as Lahar, was for us, for one afternoon at least, a little bit of heaven.

We stayed at anchor for another two days, but though we kept a constant watch, the bumboats never returned, and we reverted to our two dollops of pap per day.

On September 8 we were joined by two more cargo ships and a new escort, and continued on our way up the channel. While at the start of the voyage it had been too hazardous to sail by day, now it seemed that night spelt greater danger. As soon as dusk fell our little convoy dropped anchor. We thought that perhaps we now lay out of range of the bombers but, instead, became a target for submarines.

Next day found us making another dash across open sea, heading, if our guess was right, for the southernmost tip of the south-west tentacle of the Celebes. We made land safely, and again dropped anchor for the night. Next morning we swung north, keeping close to a well cultivated shore with numerous coconut plantations and occasional kampongs strung along a beach of blindingly white sand.

On September 12 we arrived at Macassar, and I was able to tell completely indifferent shipmates that this was where the oil with which Victorian gents plastered their hair came from, a practice which had driven Victorian wives to invent the chairback covers that came to be known as antimacassars. As we entered the port I wished that that had been allowed to remain my only recollection of the place. Two Nips on the quayside waited to catch our mooring ropes. Otherwise this gateway to the capital city of the Celebes seemed deserted. The Macassarites had apparently learned and taken to heart that first commandment for staying alive in wartime: "Thou shalt not hang around docks." Our skipper, too, seemed to be of the same persuasion. After a gang of reluctant coolies had been rounded up to bring aboard supplies of vegetables, dried fish and meat, an operation which we watched with greedy interest, he quickly got the ship under weigh, but only to anchor well offshore.

We paid another flying visit to the docks the next day for the Nips to take on board more of their precious petrol barrels. Then, after another night at anchor, we set out across the Macassar Strait in the general direction of Borneo.

At about noon the following day we dropped anchor off misty shore which we learned was the island of Pulau Laut, off Borneo's south-west tip. We were too far out to be able to see anything of the land. There we seemed to take root. Days dragged by without any sign of our voyage being resumed. A few bumboats appeared out of the mists. Again our indulgent Nips allowed us to buy mangoes, coconuts and even some fish and meat to supplement our twice-daily pap. These little luxuries came too late for some of the more seriously ill. A burial at sea became part of our morning routine. The death roll for the voyage quickly reached double figures and kept on rising.

Then the ship ran out of drinking water. And you get bloody thirsty if you've nothing to drink four degrees from the Equator. Next the galley's wood ran out and we couldn't cook. Ships came and ships went but our two boats remained obstinately at anchor. Twelve days we stagnated at this steamy anchorage. We believed we must be awaiting an escort, but none ever came. At last, on the morning of September 27, we upped anchor and started the dash over the final stretch of open sea.

We sighted land and comparative safety on the evening of the next day. The following dawn found us sailing thankfully along the shores of the island of Madura. By 4 p.m. we were back where we had started from nearly eighteen months earlier: Surabaya docks.

The return from the islands had been quite a journey. As we laughed at one another perched bare-arsed on the ship's outrigger loo, or joked over the share-out of the fat weevil grubs in the pap, eighty of the 500 men who had boarded the two ships died. And yet we were lucky. We realised just how lucky when survivors of the next two ships to leave Ambon arrived in Java. Their stories were confused and sometimes contradictory, but it became clear that next to leave Ambon after us were a party of 150 who set out on October 9. Their troubles began when they were caught by bombers off Macassar. Six men were killed and several injured. The ship was so badly damaged that even the Nips decided it had to be abandoned. The survivors were picked up by a second ship, already crammed with 600 prisoners, which had left Ambon on October 19.

This hellship remained at anchor off Macassar for no fewer than 43 interminable days, while starving men waited desperately for their two rations of watery pap, 43 terrible days in which 150 men died, one of them my old friend Sid. Just how appalling conditions became on this floating charnel house defies description. Those who survived told how sharks waited by the ship for their daily feast, and how the bodies were seen to be torn apart before they had time to sink. The 750 men who sailed on these two ships had stayed behind when we left Ambon because they were supposedly fitter men. Yet in all 309 of them died on that terrible voyage.

15: JAM ON IT

October, 1944 - January, 1945.   Makasura, Java

Our tremendous relief on returning safely to Java could not be dimmed even by the guards who cuffed us off the boat at Surabaya. Here the Nips were their old self-confident selves, demonstrating their devotion to Emperor and country by being brutal to us prisoners. It was obvious that the war had largely by-passed Java. Crowds, even in the dock area, calmly ambled about their business as though the bomber had never been invented.

We were half-expecting, even hoping, to go back to Jaarmarkt when we were herded into the station. We remembered the short rail trip from near the camp to the docks after Bluebeard's "The Nipponese army will protect you" speech on our way to the islands.

But this time we stayed in the carriages nearly forty-eight hours. They weren't exactly first class, but after Ambon and the boat, we found them sheer luxury. We lolled around in exhausted stupor on our wooden benches, stirring only to collect the rice, tea and, unbelievably, bread, served up at one or two of the dozens of stops along the line. We travelled at snail's pace, east to west, almost the full length of Java's north coast. But we felt no compulsion to find out what awaited us at the end of the line. So far as we were concerned the journey could have gone on forever. It eventually ended at 10 a.m. on October 1, when our train steamed into Batavia.

Lorries awaited the sick, and a march of unspecified length awaited the so-called fit. I was somewhere in between. Though my ankle remained painful, I had been able to hobble around for some days. The obvious answer seemed to be to hang on to my "sick" label and climb on to a lorry. But experience had shown that where the Nips were concerned it was seldom healthy to be sick, particularly if they thought you weren't. What's more there was no guarantee that the lorries would reach the same destination as the marchers, and I didn't want to be split off from the main party.

I hesitated. After two years in which my life had been directed for me down to the smallest details, I felt incapable of making a decision, and dithered. The lorries filled up and moved off, and I was left standing. For better or worse I faced the march, or, as it turned out, the crawl, to our new camp. Many of us proved so weak that even the usual encouragements by the Nip escort could not hurry us. Mercifully we had only a couple of miles to go, and I survived the ordeal reasonably well.

Makasura camp came as a shock. Its cleanliness and orderliness rocked us back on what remained of our rubber heels. We were immediately put into quarantine so as not to contaminate its residents. The Nips, or perhaps the Aussie hierarchy who seemed to run this amazing camp, decided that we must undergo a course of de-lousing, de-bugging and cleaning up before being released for general circulation. But, with the luxury of a piped water supply and ample accommodation in well-built huts, even solitary confinement would have been a pleasure.

And the menu in this Pow Hilton bordered on the fantastic. On our first morning we were astonished to be presented with a hunk of bread with our breakfast pap. Not perhaps the sort of bread your friendly neighbourhood baker would be proud of, but a fair attempt nevertheless. And as our memories of crusty cottage loaves were becoming rather dim, no-one complained, particularly as it was served with a dab of jam. Then for lunch we devoured rice with a glorious veg stew containing real meat. And at night we found rice, that stew again and another piece of that wonderful bread. And this wasn't Christmas or the Emperor's birthday, just a normal day's fare! Of course there could have been more generous helpings, but then there could have been champagne and caviare too.

We saw no work, no sign of Nips, not a thing to worry us. Someone suggested we must have died and reached that gigantic Pow camp in the sky. But acute stomach troubles due to the suddenly improved diet brought us quickly down to earth again.

My problems began when the camp's social security officials, or whatever guardian angels had now taken over the direction of our lives, decreed that we of the Ambon group, as we were now designated, must each receive half a kilo of sugar. It didn't look much like those mini diamonds dispensed by Tate and Lyle, more like sand. But I tried a bit on the tip of my finger. Not bad. In fact the incredibly intense sweetness simply intoxicated me. Diamonds or not, it was a real treasure, to be stored carefully and used sparingly.

After delicate negotiations with a better-equipped acquaintance, I acquired a rusty old syrup tin complete with lid. I poured my sugar into it and stowed it away under my pillow, or whatever was acting as a pillow at the time.

I spent the next half hour in dreamy anticipation of the pleasure of sweet drinks to come. No need to use more than half a teaspoonful at a time. I could make it last for weeks. On second thoughts, perhaps I could allow myself just one teaspoonful neat as a special treat. Then I'd forget about it. But who could have forgotten the sheer bliss of that first spoonful? Not me I'm afraid. I stuck it out for twenty minutes then I was back in the tin for just one more special treat. All that afternoon I fought a losing battle against the irresistible urge for just another taste. The intervals between them became shorter and shorter. By evening the tin was empty, and I was beginning to feel sick, very sick.

That night, as I retched and retched, I cursed myself for my stupidity. Who but an utter idiot would have wasted his precious sugar and made himself ill into the bargain? I was so ill that I couldn't even arouse much enthusiasm when a wild rumour went round the huts that we were to be issued with Red Cross parcels. Judging by the effect of the sugar I felt that a parcel would almost certainly prove fatal.

For once rumour did blossom into fact, but any danger of over-indulgence was obviated by the limiting of the hand-out to one parcel for every six men. This limit, it appeared, was not governed by shortage of supply, but by the Nips' positive embarrassment at the very idea of food parcels.

In the first place they had every reason to prefer half-starved prisoners to well-fed, fighting fit men who could easily become a problem. Furthermore they thought the parcels much too good for us. They believed, and certainly wanted their own troops to believe, that anyone who allowed himself to be captured deserved to starve. And, in any case, they could hardly be expected to welcome the supply to prisoners of delicacies the civilian population, and even their own troops, could not get.

However, even at one among six, the arrival of the small plain cardboard boxes brought magic, a sort of nostalgic Christmas atmosphere, into our huts. They brought a problem too. A happy problem, but nevertheless a tricky one. Like any issue of food in a prison camp they had to be shared out with meticulous care, and I don't suppose it had occurred to the Red Cross when they made up the parcels that their contents should be readily divisible into sixths. The discussions proved difficult and protracted, but, after all, no-one was going anywhere. In the end, everyone received a major item and a minor item, and what couldn't be divided went to the cookhouse to pep up the rations.

My share was a small tin of bully beef and a piece of chocolate. And, having learned my lesson, I didn't eat either all at once. I joined a tins pool with three friends. Between us we opened and shared out one tin a day, spreading our feast over four days. I managed to arrange things so that my tin was the last to be opened, giving me three days to hold the smooth, cool tin of real meat in my hands like a miser with his gold. Only a month or two earlier, I reminded myself, a man had died over a tin of meat much inferior to this. The parcels did wonders for our morale. Here was a tangible link with home, and a reassurance that someone, somewhere was trying to do something on our behalf.

At length we were released from quarantine and introduced, inevitably, to the camp square. But not for working parade, nor to be harangued by the Nips, nor even to have our heads and feet counted.

The square, like everything else about this remarkable camp, had that little extra. On a pole in one corner was a two-horned loudspeaker, connected presumably with a record player. It blared out a slow repetitive tune, played on something like a bugle. I think that at the time the whole of the Nips' Greater East Asia touched its toes to the same music.

However nobody expected us to be gymnasts. Swollen with beri-beri though we were, it still came as a shock to discover just how weak we had become. For us the tune became "Music While You Walk," and half an hour just strolling backwards and forwards across the square left us utterly exhausted.

But while walking constituted a problem, we could still talk. And now we had the run of the camp we soon started to swap experiences with the privileged regular residents. The large contingent of Aussies had made full use of their enviable talent for organising things to their own advantage. Somehow or other they seemed to have got even the Nip camp commandant eating out of their hands. They had built up a fantastic prison camp, and we were delighted to share it with them. The bread we enjoyed so much came from the camp's Aussie-run oven. It was made from a flour conjured up out of what remained of copra after the oil had been extracted, tapioca and a little maize. The veg for those wonderful stews came from the camp's Aussie-run gardens. We were told you could almost see the kangkung, a Javanese creeper, growing as you watched.

Another remarkable feature of the camp was the occasional appearance of a few copies of an English-language newspaper, *The Japan Times*. For the most part it comprised rather dreary and highly suspect reports of Nip triumphs around the Pacific. Not only did we doubt whether the reported victories had actually taken place, but our geography of the area was so sadly lacking that we often didn't know where the places mentioned were, or indeed whether they existed.

What we really were interested in were the fillers dropped in where the main stories fell short. These included some fascinating stories of the heroism and devotion of the Nip fighter pilots. One resourceful flier, for instance, having taken on twelve Superfortresses singlehanded, found his ammo exhausted after shooting down the first eleven. Undaunted, he polished off the twelfth by bombarding it with the rice and veg balls his cookhouse had issued as his day's rations.

My favourite story, however, concerns a Navy O pilot who found himself in the very same frustrating situation. Eleven bombers down, one to go and no shells left. Worse still he had apparently eaten his rice balls, for he had to crash into the remaining Superfort to destroy it. In doing so he lost his undercarriage: presumably he was flying a substandard plane. Undeterred, he flew dutifully back to his base.

At this point even John Wayne might have considered baling out. But not Sakimoto. He knew that his plane was vital in the crusade against the wicked West and must not be sacrificed. Luckily he had taken his samurai sword with him on the sortie. He withdrew it from its scabbard, hacked a hole in the floor of his cockpit, pushed his legs through and landed the precious plane with his feet.

After that gem any other story must be an anticlimax, but perhaps I might just mention another hero whom even death failed to deflect from his duty. He was riddled with bullets (flukey shots no doubt) and very dead, after an epic dogfight over the Pacific. But hours later, long after the plane had run out of fuel, it returned to base and made a perfect landing. The dead pilot's unquenchable spirit, said the newspaper, had returned his blood-drenched machine ready for another brave gladiator to take up on the next mission.

We thought that behind these crazy kamikaze capers there must be a real hero, perhaps a Pow, who, forced to churn out Nip propaganda, was turning the paper into a comic with his hilarious fillers. But not so, I was assured later. These were genuine straight-faced Nip morale boosters.

On November 4 came my personal morale-booster, a letter from home, in fact nine of them. All had been written within six months, late in 1943 and early 1944. In contrast to that one letter that had somehow sneaked through to me in Haruku, this was regulation dehumanised Pow mail. Each letter contained the family address, the date and 25 more words in cold block capitals.

It was wonderful to be assured that the family were all well, but heart-rending to read my mother's despairing words in the earlier letters. Then one, dated January 1, 1944, announced that they had received their first news of me for over 18 months, official notification that I was a prisoner of war. Thereafter the letters became a little less desperate. These letters, together with the one received in Haruku, were the only mail I received in three and a half years as a Pow.

Of course the pleasure of receiving these messages from home was inevitably tinged with sadness, bringing into focus as it did all that we were missing. But at least our families were relatively safe. In many cases those of our Dutch fellow-prisoners had themselves been interned not far away in Batavia. I counted my blessings when a party of Dutchmen were taken away by the Kempetai, the Nip Gestapo. Their crime had been trying to get in touch with their wives.

As soon as we had recovered a little strength, we had to face working-parties again. But, being still very weak, I managed to get one of the much sought-after jobs in the gardens, which seemed to stretch in all directions around the camp, that supplied not only our needs, but also those of the internment camps in the town. I watered, manured and observed for myself the prodigious growth of the Java veg. An Aussie who rather surprisingly possessed a ruler claimed that one kangkung stalk grew 15 centimetres in 24 hours. Despite my efforts in the gardens, the camp food began to deteriorate both in quality and quantity. It had just been too good to be true. Then the Nips said we had been too extravagant with the wood we used for cooking. We stopped boiling water and sacrificed tea. They still weren't satisfied. It became more and more difficult to cook our food properly. But these still seemed pinpricks, after the islands: this was still comparatively paradise. We prayed fervently that we might be allowed to await the end of the war in Makasura.

Christmas arrived, our third as prisoners. We had a day off work and, having robbed ourselves of wood and rice over the previous fortnight, had a satisfying meal. But not much Yuletide spirit prevailed. Twice before we had made the best of a Pow Christmas, assuring each other that we should be out for the next one. This time no-one seemed to have much heart for another season of phoney optimism. On the other hand we didn't feel too downhearted, but simply took a sober view of our situation. So sober that my diary entry for December 31 reads like the report from the chairman of a none-too-successful company. Quite fatuously it says: "1944 has been a year of difficulties but they have been surmounted and I can look forward to the New Year with confidence. I am in reasonably good health. The war situation is definitely better than ever. This camp seems fairly settled and provides reasonably good food and treatment."

Meanwhile we received an update on the war situation from the Dutch prisoners who, mercifully, returned intact from their interrogation in the town jail. They said some Aussie airmen they had met there had assured them that the war in Europe had ended in October and that the British fleet had now entered the Pacific.

Then came the local news. It started as a whispered rumour around the huts but soon emerged as cold fact. The camp had been ordered to provide a big draft for Saigon. The idea of another sea voyage, with goodness knew what horrors to follow if you were lucky enough to survive the journey, appealed to no-one. One or

Artist-author Leo Rawlings who worked on the Burma railway, entitled this picture "Will It Never End?" (1949) which admirably sums up the feelings of the Haruku survivors when told they were being shipped out to work in Indo-China

two men even hacked at their feet with chunkels in the hope of injuring themselves just enough to avoid the draft. Most of us just left it to fate. We reasoned that, if there were any justice, the camp's long-term residents, much the fitter and stronger, would be on the boat.

But of course there was no justice, and on January 8 a thousand of us, almost entirely survivors from the islands, received a rice-and-veg ball apiece and boarded a train for the docks. Admittedly there was a sprinkling of Aussies among us. We could only assume that these outcasts had committed some unspeakable crime against their fellow-countrymen to find themselves doomed to join us.

Mercifully that slow boat to China we so much dreaded did not materialise. Instead we found ourselves boarding a fairly respectable-looking OSK ferry run by a Japanese steamship company. It was carrying civilian passengers, which seemed a good omen, and was bound, according to a fifthhand rumour, only as far as Singapore. Our spirits sagged a little as our guards crammed more and more of us into a small space beneath the afterdeck. To get all 1000 of us in, we protested, was utterly impossible. But, as we reminded ourselves yet again, there was no such word in the Nip vocabulary. By shoving, shouting and kicking, the guards proved their point. Of course they expected us to sleep standing up. When the boat sailed we were allowed long spells on deck. Two meals a day came up regularly on time: pap in the morning, but steamed rice with a spoonful of stew at night. We muttered mutinously among ourselves while thanking God that things were no worse.

We had a few tense moments four days out. A formation of Superforts was spotted heading straight for the ship. Bells clanged, orders were yelled out, and we were shoved hastily below decks. There we huddled together, listening intently to the uproar above and offering up a prayer or two. The crash of exploding bombs never came. The planes flew straight on over us as though they had never seen the sitting duck below them. We gathered later that they had already dropped their load on Singapore. The tension soon eased and only a few hours later we sailed smoothly into the very docks I had left so ignominiously nearly three years earlier.

The civilian passengers disembarked. We anxiously awaited our turn. Though it had been a luxury cruise by Nip standards, Singapore was quite far enough. We didn't fancy our chances were we to sail out into the China Sea, swarming, we firmly believed, with Yankee warships. At last, with an overwhelming feeling of relief, we received the order to move, and dragged ourselves down the gangway to the comparative safety of dry land.

16: BACK TO THE HAPPY WORLD

January - April, 1945. River Valley, Singapore

Although I realised that Singapore must be as popular a bombing target with the Allies as it had once been for the Nips I was taken aback at the scene that met me as I stepped ashore. Where once swinging cranes, bulging godowns and ships of all shapes and sizes had provided the backcloth to a dockland clutter of scurrying humanity, now I saw only acres of flat, bare, antiseptic concrete, with scarcely any sign of life, shrouded in unbelievable silence. All we could see afloat were two insignificant little coasters and a stray U-boat with the Nazi swastika fluttering forlornly at her masthead.

I would have been happy to be disembarking anywhere just to get on dry land but, despite its new look, I was particularly pleased to be in Singapore. In my spell there, before the Nips had ruined things, I had become fairly well acquainted with the city. And somehow, as we emerged from the dock area, the old familiar sights, to say nothing of the smells, gave me the feeling, quite irrationally perhaps, that I was one step nearer home.

As we trudged through the hot, sweaty streets, weighed down with our packs, I gradually became aware that we were following a familiar route. We were heading, ironically, for the Happy World. This big, gaudy Chinese amusement park, along with its competitors, the New World and the Great World, had provided many a famous, and infamous, night out in what had now become "the good old days."

But now the bizarre sideshows, the not-exactly-fragrant open-air restaurants, the cabaret with the taxi-dancers you hired for a quickstep or a waltz, were no more. The Happy World, in keeping with the times, lay derelict. But not quite as derelict as the River Valley Pow camp next door, which proved to be our destination. The atap huts, each with two tiers of sleeping platforms down both sides of a narrow gangway, were falling to pieces. Only two were occupied. From the remainder we picked out those with the least holes in the roofs, and moved in, hoping it would keep fine for us.

Our neighbours in the two occupied huts turned out to be a couple of hundred British soldiers back in Singapore after working on what was to become the notorious Burma railway. They came running to greet us as soon as our guards had left, and gave us an instant inferiority complex. They looked disgustingly fit, apparently never shorn of their hair; they had a reasonable amount of flesh on their bones, and generally made us look like scarecrows.

But though they had not faced starvation, or at least not on our level, they had had to contend with cholera. They told horrific tales of the epidemic which had brought wholesale death to the railway's Pow battalions.

They also gave us a rundown of life in Singapore under the Nips. It was hardly the gay, pulsating city of old. Syonan, as the Nips had renamed it, was very much occupied territory. That nonsense about freeing Asians from Western tyrants didn't cut much ice here. This overwhelmingly Chinese city had never had any illusions about the Nips. At last we were in a town where the locals were very much on our side, whenever they dared show it. As for the city itself, that one-time shrine of British colonial snobbery, the Raffles Hotel, was now the Nip headquarters. The YMCA, an occasional calling-place on my days off in the old days, was now occupied by the torture squads of the Kempetai.

Then there was that U-boat. Its crew, like all good Nazis, no doubt patriotically hated their British enemy, but it seemed they hated their Nip allies a damned sight more. A bunch of them, we were told, happened to be passing a docks working party as a Nip was beating up a British prisoner. They rushed over and, to the delight of the prisoners, gave the Nip a taste of his own medicine.

Our River Valley neighbours also had a few words to say about Changi, the old Singapore jail that was later to become a symbol of Nip bestiality to prisoners. Most of the tens of thousands of Britons trapped at the fall of Singapore had been sent out to different parts of the Nip empire as coolie labour. The rump had stayed on at Changi. And, having the advantage of a permanent camp, they had got themselves fairly well organised. So much so that the Burma railway chaps dubbed them the Changi pensioners.

But there was nothing permanent about River Valley. Our new friends told us it was now merely a transit camp. We were all awaiting a boat to Saigon, where apparently there were plenty of vacancies for willing, or unwilling, coolies.

We soon had evidence that, after that brief period of peace in Batavia, we were now back in a war zone. For a week or two the only excitement was the occasional reconnaissance plane or a hit-and-run raid by one or two bombers: all quite insignificant. But on February 1 the Allies showed that they really meant business.

After being plumb in the middle of the target area during so many previous raids, we felt reasonably safe in the middle of the city. Not that we were naive enough to think that the Yanks, or the British for that matter, would think twice about blasting civilians, prisoners, or anyone else if it suited their purpose. But there were few worthwhile military targets in the town, and it would have been counter-productive to terrorise the pro-Allies Chinese.

So at last we had an air raid we could enjoy. We sat outside our huts in the sun watching happily as wave after wave of planes droned in from the west to blast targets on the north side of Singapore island, chiefly, we thought, the former British naval base. It was heartening to see that the heavy ack-ack barrage was completely ineffective, and even more so to note the total absence of any fighter resistance. We did spot two Nip planes, but they kept well away from the action. We concluded that they were in the air merely to escape destruction on the ground.

For a brief interlude we had felt quite blasé about bombs, but proof that deep down we were still scared to death came later that afternoon. Our guards watched in astonishment as prisoners came hurtling through the sides of their huts in their hundreds to flatten themselves in the ditches outside, for there had been no air-raid warning, no sound of aircraft, and outside the barbed wire the city was going unconcernedly about its business.

I had been dozing on my allotted stretch of bamboo when I heard a swishing noise, and looked up to find everyone around me leaping for cover. Panic gripped me and I followed the herd. It was only when we were all wallowing in the king-size drainage ditches that it dawned on us that there was no reason whatsoever for our lemming-like behaviour. The swishing noise I had heard had nothing to do with bombs. It was the sound of bodies hurtling through the atap. What originally set the snowball of fear rolling, we never discovered.

Next morning we had something more tangible to worry about. We heard that there was a boat in the docks ready to take us to Saigon. By this time there were 3000 of us in River Valley, and, even by Nip loading standards, there was room on the ship for only 2500. We waited anxiously to hear who would be the winners and losers in the resultant lottery of misery. This turned out to be one of those times in life when those on whom Fate smiled missed the boat. Happily I was one of the lucky 500.

The draft included our friends from the Burma railway and all Dutch and Eurasian prisoners. In addition, a small group was sent off to take up vacancies among the Changi pensioners. That left 450 of us at River Valley, presumably to await the next boat.

Weeks passed. No boat arrived. Life settled down into the familiar routine, with normal near-starvation rations, the food of Makasura no more than a dream. We resumed our usual rôle as coolies to the Nip army, specialising in hole-digging and road-mending, but with one very welcome difference from all our previous work experience: most of the jobs involved a march through city streets.

Since that night arrival in Surabaya from Semarang, in the far distant past, when we had caught glimpses through lighted windows of families gathering for their evening meal, we had seen very few of what you might call ordinary folk: hardly anyone except Nips and fellow prisoners. So it was a real pleasure to be almost rubbing shoulders in the streets with old folk, young folk, whole families leading ordinary lives... as ordinary, that is, as the Nips would let them.

We received a warm smile, and a friendly word too if our guards were not paying too much attention. At last we heard at first hand news from the great world outside. We learned details, for instance, of the many casualties and heavy damage caused by the February 1 raid, carried out, we were now told, by 90 Calcutta-based B29s.

When our new friends started talking of what "it said in the papers" we felt we really had returned from the limbo of the East Indies. Civilisation lay just on the other side of the barbed wire. Even Calcutta had a homely ring about it after life had been centred for so long on Java.

Soon there were more air raids to discuss. February 21 brought a heavy road on the dock area. Then on February 24 oil installations on the off-shore island of Blakang Mati were hit. A huge pall of black smoke blotted out the sun, and the fire burned for days. Again there had been no sign of any Nip fighters. It was all becoming a playback of February 1942, but with reverse rôles. The Allies ruled the skies, bombing with impunity. The Nips shivered in their shelters, utterly impotent. Only one thing was unchanged: we remained on the receiving end.

With mixed feelings I found myself a few days later in a working party on its way to unload a ship at the docks. Of course ships could mean food, but docks generally spelt trouble. This occasion was no exception. The ship was loaded with cement, in hundredweight bags, all torn and leaking. And worse than the cement bags were the Nips who went with them.

We had often speculated whether it was working on docks that turned Nips into fiends, or whether there was a particularly vicious type of Nip bred specially for the job. Whatever the case we encountered a bunch of what I can only describe as absolute bastards. These squat, evil little gnomes with wicked tempers, and wicked bamboo poles to match, drove us, coughing and spluttering, through suffocating clouds of cement into the hold. Then, as we staggered back on the deck beneath our leaky bags, half-blinded and with spilt cement congealing on our sweating bodies, there they were again, eagerly waiting to make us run the gauntlet on to the dockside. No sooner had we dumped our bags than they were pushing us back down the hold again, unceasingly. This purgatory continued all day. And there's precious little edible to pinch on a cement ship.

Work at the docks became part of our regular pattern of life. Mercifully there weren't many cement ships, but there was seldom anything much more appetising either. So we had to look elsewhere. And, still standing among the general desolation, were a couple of storage tanks rather like mini gasholders. Desperation drove someone to crawl through an outlet pipe into a tank. He found that though it had been emptied, remnants of its last load of palm oil still clung to its sides. He came out with a sample.

One of the more knowledgeable of our party said it was used to make soap, and it tasted like it. But when he added that it was full of vitamins, he started a sort of palm oil Klondyke. We all crawled into the tanks to fill our mess-tins. We took the orange coloured glue back to camp and put it on our evening rice. It didn't do much for the taste, but it didn't do any harm either. Soon no day on the docks was complete without a visit to the tanks.

The docks provided me with one other delicacy. One yasmay period, while inspecting some weeds for edibility, I discovered four giant slugs. Not very appetising, but I felt sure they must contain some desperately-needed protein. It was a chance I couldn't afford to miss. If the French could eat snails, I could eat slugs. I toasted them gently over a fire to get rid of the slime, and then popped them gingerly into my mouth. When it came to chewing them, however, my stomach revolted. But I wasn't going to give up now. I spat them out again, cut them into swallowable pieces, and gulped them down.

With Greater East Asia falling to bits all around them, the Nips began to lose a little of their bounce. It was a long while since we had heard anything of the "We're not afraid to die. We'd never be taken prisoner" brigade.

There was certainly no mistaking the change of tune among the Koreans. It was difficult to believe that those running the River Valley camp were of the same race as the Bull and his friends at Jaarmarkt, who had taken such a positive delight in humiliating us. After three years at the bottom of the Nip army slapping order and perhaps now thinking a Nip defeat could mean their country's independence, the River Valley Koreans now claimed they wanted to be our friends. They whispered that the Nips would try to kill us when the end came, and promised to do all they could to warn us and help us escape. Meanwhile they no longer badgered us around the camp and even claimed to be trying to wangle us extra rations.

Quite a number of the Nips who took us out working seemed to have lost a great deal of their enthusiasm for chasing us around, and, as a result, our chances of contact with the Chinese in the streets were considerably improved. Almost daily a little tobacco or some cooked rice in a banana leaf would be pressed into some lucky prisoner's hand. Street traders would leave titbits on a corner of their stalls where we could grab them as we passed.

Unfortunately these little kindnesses led to one to two incidents which, in retrospect, I can only describe as shameful. But I'm afraid an empty belly has little conscience.

167

On one occasion, for instance, a party of 50 men, shepherded by a couple of particularly indulgent Nips, happened to pass a stall selling sun-dried fish. As usual there were two fish waiting to be picked up. The first two lucky men grabbed them. But that left 48 unlucky, and this time hunger got the better of any sense of fair play. Everyone wanted some and in the melée that followed the stall was completely cleared of everything on it.

Our Nips preferred to see nothing and say nothing. We marched happily on, stuffing stolen fish down our shorts, and leaving at least one Oriental more than a little disillusioned about Western standards of behaviour.

Not surprisingly, after one or two smash-and-grab raids of this sort, the stall-holders developed the unfortunate, if understandable, habit of clearing everything edible well out of reach the moment one of our columns was sighted.

The stallholders weren't our only victims. I remember well my working party overtaking a street trader with a large tin of crisps strapped to his back. He was quite happy for one or two of us to help ourselves to a handful as we passed, but looked decidedly agitated when he emerged from a scrum of jostling bodies with his tin empty.

Despite our lapses, the Chinese remained on good terms. In three years of often brutal suppression by the Nips they had faced problems much worse than a few light-fingered Pows. The last trouble, they told us, was roaring inflation. The Nips had printed and issued large quantities of notes wherever their troops had landed. The value of this currency had plunged with the Nips' fortunes of war, rapidly becoming worthless.

Our friends looked happier after March 2 when 50 or 60 bombers turned up to hammer the naval base yet again. They told us gleefully that three warships had been sunk, including an aircraft-carrier said to have been sliced in half.

The Chinese had cheering news too from farther afield. British troops had taken Mandalay and were pushing on to Rangoon while island-hopping Americans were said to have cut Nippon off from her ill-gotten empire. Surely the end could not be far off.

So far as we were concerned there was one big snag. Singapore began to run out of food. On March 3 our rice ration diminished to 300 grams per day for outside workers, 250 for other allegedly fit men and 200 for the unfortunate sick. Our only other food was

'Banana money' as the Singapore Chinese called it, which rolled off the Nip presses in the occupied territories without even serial numbers. Its value gradually became less and less until it was declared worthless at the end of the war

a few greens and a minute quanitity of dried fish. Even the outside worker, the élite of Pow society, had to survive on two meals of watery pap morning and midday with a small portion of steamed rice and veg soup at night. The others received proportionately less, but somehow they seemed to survive.

Any Nip who had not had his senses beaten out of him by the army's savage discipline could now see that the Greater East Asia dream had turned into a nightmare. The only course open was to start digging, or start the prisoners digging. We now concentrated on three jobs, all on holes and tunnels.

Our biggest contract was on the Bukit Timah Road at the former Chinese Girls' High School, which now had Nip army cadets as its pupils. We had already slung up a defensive wall around it, and next set to work tunnelling into a hill to carve out what we believed to be an underground operations room. The work proved tough and dangerous, but surprisingly with little of the usual bullying and beatings. Many of the cadets spoke excellent English. I recalled that other English-speaking Nip at

Semarang, who had informed us that we were not prisoners, but guests of the Emperor. Well, the cadets didn't bring on the geisha girls, in fact they kept us hard at it, but they did keep their guests well supplied with buckets of thick sweet coffee. And that coffee, thanks no doubt to a sugar-starved palate, seemed the best I had ever tasted.

Back at camp, our tame Koreans bolstered our rising hopes of an early Allied victory. They said 1400 American ships were converging on Southern Nippon. In the north the Russians had made threatening noises towards Tokyo. But the Koreans' promise to help us when the big crunch came would never be put to the test. They had one last item of news for us: we were to be moved from River Valley.

After the talk of an Allied armada in the South China Sea we prayed that our boat had not come in. But we needn't have worried. When, on April 10, we collected our tins and rags together and dragged ourselves out of the camp, we ended up only a mile or two across town at Tanjong Pagar, near the docks. Not good, but certainly better than sailing to Saigon.

17: THEN CAME THE BOMB

April - September, 1945. Tanjong Pagar, Singapore

The Tanjong Pagar camp was already occupied by 600 prisoners from Java, including a number of Aussies, when we arrived. The guards were again reformed Koreans, but this lot were under the watchful eye of a Nip sojo. He certainly had not yet seen the light, and appeared quite impervious to Aussie manipulation.

Under the taciturn sojo, our food deteriorated even more. The outside worker's 300 gram of rice sank to little more than 200. We suspected the sojo of flogging our rations to black marketeers in the town. Weak as we were, many of us began to feel appreciably weaker, some suffering spells of dizziness. We kept complaining, and eventually received a little tapioca to supplement the rice. It didn't help much, but fortunately our new work, cleaning up the docks, gave some opportunity for stealing. With shipping at a standstill, we found little about, but occasionally knocked off a little rice or sugar. Those who were caught suffered severe beatings, but we were too desperate to stop. A few lucky ones caught and ate rats.

We still gleaned palm oil scrapings from the tanks, but our enthusiam for its nutritional value had waned, and we now put it to its proper use. Under the guidance of the camp boffins we mixed it with wood ash from the cookhouse fires and produced something resembling soap. This was a luxury indeed, but you can't eat soap, and we felt convinced we were slowly but surely starving to death.

However, it seemed the Nips did not wish us to die, at least not while they had work for us. And to keep us alive they decided on drastic action. On April 10 they generously let us have some of our Red Cross parcels, not one between six this time, but one between two. Apart from that tantalising taste of paradise on our return to Java from the islands, this was the first Red Cross food we had seen in three years in the bag, which certainly wasn't the fault of the Red Cross. They had overcome tremendous difficulties to get their parcels through to the other side of a war-torn world, but even they couldn't force the local Nips to hand them over. Rather than let us have them, the Singapore Nips simply stacked the embarrassing packages in some secret store. Perhaps they had reckoned that sooner or later pilferers would solve the distribution problems. But now, when they couldn't feed us and they needed our labour, the time had come for them to make a benevolent gesture.

Whatever the reason, we got our precious cardboard boxes. And few parcels can ever have been more needed or more appreciated. They were in excellent condition, the familiar labels on the individual items being a tonic in themselves. Each box contained 15 or 16 items: a tin of meat, a pudding, some margarine, sugar, sweets and so on. Perhaps you could have bought the lot for five bob in England, but in Singapore they were priceless, and certainly much too valuable to be consumed all at one go. So, as in Makasura, we pooled our treasures, using, for instance, one tin of meat between four. In this way, we transformed every evening meal into a veritable banquet for the next week or more. This changed the whole atmosphere of the camp: suddenly it was everyone's birthday and Christmas all rolled into one.

Unfortunately the feast couldn't last for ever, and we were soon back on basic rations, reflecting sadly how much more comfortable it would be to await the end of the war with full bellies.

Early in May we sensed that something momentous was happening from the way our guards, both in camp and on working parties, kept gathering in little huddles for animated discussions. We couldn't catch their drift, but anything that directed their attention away from us couldn't be all bad.

On May 10 our camp guards came out with it. This time it was no whispered rumour. A formal announcement was made on the morning tenko parade that Germany had surrendered on the seventh. We remained a little sceptical, failing to understand why the Nips should want to tell us what, for them, must obviously be shattering news. For us it seemed too good to be true.

But as we marched outside the camp gates to work, the Chinese in the streets, absolutely unable to contain themselves, Nips or no Nips, shouted at us that the war in Europe had indeed ended. In the docks we saw the U-boat's swastika ensign had been replaced by the Nip navy's rising sun. We were convinced.

In our mood of general euphoria, we decided the Nips must have broken the news to us to point out that they were now facing the whole world on their own, excusing, in advance, the defeat that even they realised must be inevitable. We dreamed of the day when we would gorge ourselves until we fell on our faces, too bloated to get up again.

As well as losing their confidence, the Nips had lost their voices. Back on the islands, particularly on their rare fiesta nights, we had listened to them belting out their war hit, "Lords of the Pacific". Occasionally the strains of "Auld Lang Syne", strangely accompanied by Nip caterwauling, would come drifting on the tropical breezes. Now they were silent.

Our own voices had become rather muted after the rousing choruses of Semarang, when we were still pinning our hopes on the rice legend prophecy of freedom after 100 days. But now, after some 1140 days, we started to sing again. We rolled out the barrel and fell in love down Mexico way as we marched through Singapore. On the way to one of our jobs, we passed the Nip naval headquarters. For them we always had a special show. Our straggling rabble miraculously sprang into presentable ranks and we swung along defiantly bawling out "Wings Over The Navy". Personally I would have preferred something British, but the American tune came easier. And, after all, it was really the Yanks we were relying on to swat the Nips.

May 30, a day long forecast by an Aussie sergeant fortune-teller as release day, passed with nothing more than an air-raid alarm. We weren't unduly put out. For us Poms, even freedom would have been slightly tarnished with an Aussie crowing "I told you so".

Not that we didn't get along all right with the Aussies. We had to. It's perhaps just that a nation that has grown out of a penal colony has constantly to be asserting itself. Our Aussies had an image they must live up to. The demanded to be seen as hard-drinking, gambling toughs. That was not easy in a prison camp. But they thought they'd found their chance one day down on the docks. They came back from a working party waving waterbottles of booze. They'd found it, they said, in an old godown.

Well, among us Poms you could generally find someone, somewhere who knew something about any subject that happened to crop up. And more than one expert identified the Aussie booze as almost certainly industrial alcohol, and poisonous. The Aussies didn't want to know. No Pom killjoy was going to ruin their first booze-up in three years. So they had their party, each man determined to drink his neighbour under the bamboo. The hangover proved brutal. Within 48 hours five men were dead, one blind, and several others seriously ill. Even our Koreans expressed astonishment at the sheer lunacy of it all. Here were men who had survived long, weary years of hardship and danger tossing their lives away just when, at long last, it seemed possible that freedom might already be steaming towards us down the Malacca Strait.

A few days later our guards appeared on tenko parade with a weighing machine. They had orders, they said, that every man must be weighed and his weight recorded. We were dumb-founded. Never before had the Nips shown any statistical interest in us other than having the right number of bodies, alive or dead. The weights were not surprising. I was 7st 5lb, against a pre-Nip weight of over 10st.

Our personal figures didn't interest us as much as the reasons for the exercise. Some theorised that the Nip top brass had begun to get a little concerned about being caught with so many starving prisoners under their command. On the other hand the more pessimistic among us suggested that they were checking on how much they could get for us at the local glue factory.

Some incurable optimists (still not quite extinct) thought that the pitiful figures might persuade the camp sojo to release the Red Cross parcels we felt convinced he was holding somewhere on the camp. Of course he didn't, or at least not to us. But he must have been fiddling with them because he gave us cocoa drinks and a little real soap that could have come from no other source.

Incongruous though it may seem, the brighter our hopes of freedom burned, the more worried I became. In the past, release had seemed so remote that I had not dwelt overmuch on whether my personal war would have a happy ending. Now I became obsessed with fears that I might be pipped on the post. I became scared that the Nips would shoot us rather than let us be repatriated, scared I might be killed in an Allied attack, and, when another prisoner died of dysentery on June 27, that disease or starvation would get me yet.

I would have been petrified had I known the kamikaze plans of the commander of Singapore, a General Itagaki. He was preparing one last act of suicidal defiance, and he didn't take us into his confidence, but when we were all switched suddenly to digging tunnels and "death before surrender" bunkers in the hills behind the docks we had our suspicions.

The work was bad enough in itself, a hammer and chisel job for dynamite charges, then shovelling out the rockfall. With the Nips under pressure from their top brass, beatings, kicking and general bullying reached a new frenzy. As usual they worked on the principle that if a job is impossible you simply pile in more bodies. The result followed the old familiar pattern, with so many of us packed into the tunnels that we got in one another's way, slowing the job down. The Nips crowded in still more men and flew into wild rages when the work ground to a standstill.

Out of this hell came a heartwarming incident which I often think about even now with gratitude and, if it doesn't sound too naive, with humility. So many men had been sent out for work in such confined spaces in so much confusion that it was often possible for ones and twos to go off foraging without being missed.

That was how one morning I found myself studying a small field with a palm-thatch house in the middle of it, and a few forlorn-looking tapioca plants growing nearby. There seemed no-one about, so I moved warily in. I tugged at the stalks of the plants in an effort to get at the edible roots. But there had been no rain for some time, the ground was like concrete, and I had made no impression on them whatever. Then the door of the hut opened. I prepared to bolt, but there was no shout of rage to bring the Nips running. Instead a middle-aged Chinese woman, drably clothed in the usual black trouser-suit, emerged to offer me a chunkel. She had apparently been watching my futile efforts and wanted to help. I took the chunkel and got cracking.

When I had dug up as many roots as I could carry, I walked over to the hut to return the chunkel. The woman reappeared in the dim entrance, bringing me a white substance. I thought it was salt, and thanked her for salt in my pidgin Malay. It wasn't; it was rice, and as she handed it over she insisted that I wait while she brought me some salt too. I mumbled my thanks. I felt embarrassed. First by the generosity this woman, probably eking out no more than a bare subsistence herself, had shown to a foreigner she had found robbing her vegetable patch. And, secondly, by her courage. For she must have been well aware that if she had been discovered by the Nips helping a prisoner, a severe beating would have been the very least she could expect. I wondered what I should have done had our rôles been reversed.

However I didn't let embarrassment spoil my appetite. As soon as the Nips called yasmay for the midday rice, I lit a fire and, with a few friends, enjoyed a substantial meal of roasted tapioca. All thanks to a kind, brave woman. The world would be a better place if there were more like her.

July crawled slowly on. An English-language newspaper was smuggled into camp. It was the *Syonan Shimbun*, a skeletal version of the old *Straits Times*. The Allies had taken Balikpapan, an important oil port not so far away in Borneo. Tokyo was being hit by increasing air raids. And this was merely what the Nips were allowing to be printed. Their position had become hopeless, but they seemed intent on national suicide.

Conditions on the bunkers got even worse. The Nips now regarded them as so important that they gave us a quarter of a tin of bully beef each from their hoard of our Red Cross parcels to keep our srength up. As we finished one bunker, another was started. We began a new set commanding the railway line heading north out of the city. It seemed the Nips now believed an invasion of Singapore to be imminent.

On August 1 a large group of us were suddenly moved out of the Tanjong Pagar camp, and marched down the road to another camp at Morse Road, outside the dock area, away from the shore but nearer to those wretched bunkers.

A few more bunkers completed, we felt, and the Nips' preparations for their fight to the death would be ready. We would be not only surplus to requirements, but a positive liability, and felt sure they must then kill us.

We would have to make a break for it. The big question was when. Too early, and the Nips would be able to give their undivided attention to hunting us down. Ideally we wanted to be sprinting for freedom while the Nips were facing up to the invading troops. But by then we might·have been dealt with.

But there was an answer to our problems coming up: perhaps the only thing that could have saved us. First it was just a whispered rumour from the Chinese about a super bomb. Then the Nips eased up on the work at the bunkers and began talking

The end of the world for thousands. Salvation for many thousands more. Artist Montague Black painted this dramatic vivid impression of the horrendous moment when the first atom bomb exploded over Hiroshima

agitatedly among themselves. Eventually they took us into their confidence. Very big bombs had been dropped on Nippon killing huge numbers of people.

They meant the Hiroshima and Nagasaki atom bombs. Suddenly, though we were not immediately aware of it, our world had undergone a dramatic transformation. Our future prospects, our very life expectancy, had been immeasurably improved.

Work continued, but without the same sense of urgency. One of the older Nips actually told us to work more "plan plan". After three and a half years of "lakas lakas", we thought he must have got his Malay words mixed up. It was inconceivable that any Nip should tell us to go slow. But he eventually convinced us that, yes, he really meant it.

A few days later a couple of the U-boat Germans, billeted not far from our Morse Road camp, happened to pass us as we were on our way to the bunkers. They yelled excitedly: "Stop working for the bastards. It's all over."

We were still working on August 15, but on our return to camp the miracles began. We were given a cup of sweet coffee and three cigarettes per man, with the promise that this would be repeated each day from now on. We continued to go through the motions of work at the bunkers, but a day or so later we were all suddenly sent back to camp at three o'clock in the afternoon. Our Korean guards announced that there would be more rice and no more work. We scarcely dared express our hopes in words in case we were to be cruelly disappointed. Then the U-boat crew came driving past our camp on the back of a lorry. They had no doubts. "The war's finished. The war's finished," they shouted, obviously delighted that their former ally had been brought to her knees.

The only people who didn't seem to be sure that peace had broken out were our camp Koreans. Their problem was that, while Tokyo had surrendered on August 14, Itagaki had decided that Singapore should fight on alone. This left our guards in a sort of limbo. Officially they were still at war, but they eased conditions for us just to be on the safe side.

On the 19th we were moved out of Morse Road back to Tanjong Pagar. As we marched down the road, the Chinese left us in no doubt of their reading of the situation. Though still keeping well out of the Nips' rifle butts, they smiled, waved and sang as we passed.

Map to show South-East Asia in August 1945

Our guards still said nothing, but lingering doubts about our new status were removed on our arrival at our huts. Each of us received a 3ft by 6ft piece of plywood to sleep on. We were definitely coming up in the world, by about three eighths of an inch anyway.

Perhaps our camp did not become a five-star hotel overnight, but suddenly we could have as much rice and sugar as we liked. There was a promise of vegetables and even fresh meat. Scraps of tinned meat appeared in our stew that very evening. By the 22nd the goodies had started to pour in. We actually received one Red Cross parcel per man, which was presumably what the Red Cross had always intended. Two pigs arrived at the cookhouse, a gift from the Singapore Chinese, who had already given us so much, not always voluntarily.

The Nips, whose only contribution to our bedding since capture had been those sheets of plywood, now came up with a blanket apiece. I use the term "blanket" loosely. I think they had

'We've made it!' A group of survivors pictured in Singapore immediately after the Nip surrender. Free, but still at Tanjong Pagar camp. Bottom left is Don Peacock

been intended for horses. Certainly they were useless for sleeping under. They were almost as stiff as the plywood. But they were indestructible. I brought mine home. For years it kept the car warm in winter and served as a picnic rug in summer. It finally disappeared after doing a stint as a dust-sheet during house decorations.

But we remained prisoners. The Koreans still manned the camp's tall bamboo sentry towers and stood guard at the gates. But for the moment we relaxed content from our past labours, lazing around on our plywood sheets and enjoying the vastly-improved meals. On the 28th Allied bombers came droning low over the city dropping leaflets to inform anyone still in doubt that peace had broken out.

On the 30th Singapore finally fell to six men of the RAMC who dropped in by parachute. My diary-writing had become somewhat slapdash by this time but I remember their driving into our camp to see if we were all right, and giving us a Union Jack. This didn't change life much, but still it was nice of them to call.

On September 4 we heard that a British warship, *HMS Cleopatra*, had arrived, but for us Freedom Day was September 5, three weeks after the official surrender. We awoke to find all the guards had disappeared. Then around lunchtime I climbed up one of the deserted sentry towers for a grandstand view of the arrival of a vast invasion fleet.

Dark storm clouds hung low over the horizon. Beneath them the sun sparkled on an arc of white flecks stretching away to the horizon. Slowly the flecks grew into long white arrows of foam. Each was the wake of a ship. Gradually the armada took shape. Landing craft led destroyers, cruisers, troopships, the lot. More ships than Singapore had seen for many a long day. It was like the grande finale of one of those old Hollywood epics where the Army, the Navy, the Air Force and Uncle Tom Cobley and all come speeding to the rescue.

I had taken the events of the past few days fairly calmly. I felt the last three and half years had pretty well drained me of emotion. But now, as I was finally convinced that I had made it, I felt a lump in my throat and tears in my eyes. The hundred days of captivity forecast in the Java rice legend had once seemed a lifetime. But I'd survived one thousand two hundred and seventy-six of them. And I would be going home after all.

181

As the fleet closed in, it split up, the landing craft heading for the islands, the bigger ships making for the docks. Then I lost sight of them all. For a while there was an eerie calm. Then, fanning out along the approaches to our camp we saw our first Allied troops, bearded Indians with fixed bayonets. They moved stealthily past the camp barbed wire, obviously taking no chances. But they found no opposition. In fact no Nips. Then, as the Indians moved on into the city, our camp was inundated with war correspondents, showering us with cigarettes as they made their notes.

We broke down the barbed fences and walked out, unescorted at last, into the road outside. In the confusion I somehow found myself, quite alone, walking down the main road into the city, wildly cheered by the thousands of Chinese who had gathered spontaneously on the streets to welcome the British troops.

This became rather embarrassing. My war record hardly made me a conquering hero. I dived down a side street, but found myself in a none too salubrious *cul de sac*. I faced the multitude for another hundred yards then tried again. This time I was more fortunate. A little ahead of me I saw a few Chinese sitting at a table enjoying a meal. It seemed to be a pavement café. There was an empty chair, so I sat down. Before I had time to say anything, I was served with a bowl of rich soup with lumps of pork floating in it. I sat back and enjoyed my first meal on the right side of the barbed wire.

As I finished, it occurred to me that there might be some difficulty. I had no money. I could only hope that the cigarettes the war correspondents had given me would pay the bill. I called over a Chinese who seemed to be waiting on, and explained my position. "Nothing to pay," he assured me cheerily. "This is a funeral."

I'm a bit hazy about the next few days. Lord and Lady Mountbatten dropped in to see us. I can remember some ENSA types begging us to watch some showbiz stars they had brought to the camp, but few wanted to stay inside the barbed wire when they had the freedom of the city outside.

We found ourselves very busy. Nip-bashing became popular, and gangs of Nips were soon doing odd jobs under guard around the city. And many of the guards were only too happy to oblige a Pow who wanted a bit of his own back. Understandable enough, but perhaps unfortunate. All the time I had been a prisoner I had felt superior to these yellow goons. To start beating them up was descending to their level.

Other ex-prisoners (what a difference an ex makes!) went out to see the Nips in their prison camps and win themselves officers' swords. No more than poetic justice that this symbol of samurai might should be reduced to a sort of holiday souvenir.

I spent a lot of time on the cruiser *Sussex* where they baked unlimited supplies of real English bread. No copra husks in these delicious slices.

I needed a certain amount of re-education before taking up the old life again. It was strange to use a sit-down toilet again after years of the Oriental squat.

Then some Navy types hijacked me to the frigate *Verulam*, anchored offshore. The *Verulam* had come out East direct from Russian convoy duty, so as well as wining and dining me lavishly, her crew presented me with Arctic-type vests and longjohns for the journey home. They were much too big but the vests kept the frost off sacks of potatoes in my shed for twenty years or more.

After this brief interlude of glorious riot in Singapore, the RAF started rounding us up. They didn't waste much time, visualising the danger of those first heady days of freedom doing as much harm as three and a half years as Pows... well almost, anyway.

'Welcome Home!' On his release, Don Peacock weighed little over seven stones, but vitamin pills pumped into him during the long voyage home had dramatic effect. This is how his father, a cartoonist with the Northern Despatch, welcomed him home to Darlington

Epilogue

It would have been understandable if the men of Haruku had blotted the island of so many bitter memories right out of their minds. But it doesn't seem to have happened. Over the years small groups of the survivors have made the long arduous journey back. They go to pay respect to lost friends whose graves are now gathered in the war cemetery in Ambon. But more than that they seem drawn irresistibly to visit once again the island that was the end of the road for so many, and perhaps in subtle ways, and sadly in some cases not so subtle, changed the lives of all who came back.

Among these pilgrims were the smiling group of seven pictured

Back to Haruku. From left to right: Fred Ryall, Bass Trevethick, Geoff Lee, Jack Russell, Tony Cowling, Tom Coles and Dave Harries

Haruku: a happier face nowadays on the island of disease, despair and death

on the Ambon Ferry. Predictably their endurance in making the trip earned them, among less venturesome friends, the title of The Magnificent Seven. They went to see not only the island but also the people, and children of people, who shared the dark days of war. The earlier pilgrims found the older folk fearful of strangers. The Nip experience was etched in their minds. The Magnificent Seven met a friendly, bright and breezy new generation and brought back some happier memories of the island of death.

A cheerful school has grown up on the old camp square where the Gunzo carried out his merciless beatings of prisoners. The Seven have helped with its books and equipment. Happily there is no trace of the Nip guardroom which once stood on the opposite side of the road.

Index

durian, 123
Dutch, in Bandung, 19, 21; women of Semarang, 32, 39–40, 48, 61-2; Pows, ix, 26-9, 32, 39, 61-2, 65, 68-9, 72, 165; troops, 9, 14, 42
dysentery, 62, 70, 82, 84-95, 104

eggs and chickens, 127, 132-5, 139, 148
Empire Star, 4-9
escapes, 98

films, 69-70
fishing, 97
food, 34, 44-5, 50-1, 55, 57, 59-61, 64-6, 75, 81-3, 85, 87-9, 92, 94, 96, 100–4, 109, 116, 125-7, 131, 139, 142, 148, 150, 153, 155, 158, 165-71, 180
football, 60
funerals, 87, 98, 104, 117, 121-2

gardens, 18
Garut, 13
Germany, surrender of, 172
goats, 88-9
'Goldie' (a Japanese), 35-9
'guests', not prisoners, 50

Happy World, Singapore, 162
Harries, Dave, 93, 137, 185
Haruku, 80-140, 157, 185-6
heroism, 17
Hirohito, *Emperor,* viii, 66, 78-9

Hiroshima, 177-8
Hitler, Adolf, 98, 109
hornets, 123-4
Hurricane aircraft, 5

Indo-China, 158
Indonesia. *See* individual islands, *e.g.* Haruku *and* individual towns, *e.g.* Tasikmalaya
informers, 106-7
Itagaki, *General,* 175, 178

Jaarmarkt, Surabaya, 64-72
Jakarta (formerly Batavia), 4, 8-9, 157, 164
Japan Times, 156
Japanese Air Force, 54-5, 58-9, 156-7, 166
Java, 4, 8-75. *See also* towns in Java, *e.g.* Semarang
'Ju Achi' (a Japanese), 123-4
Jupiter, H.M.S., 65

Kalibantan, Semarang, 34-6
Kasi Yama (a Japanese), 84, 94, 105, 122
Kempetai, 157
Koreans, 64-6, 167, 170-1, 178, 181

latrines, 18, 67, 74, 84-6, 105, 183
Lee, Geoff, 185
legends, 21
letters, 112-3, 157
Liang, 117-8, 138–40, 144-5
lice, 107-8
Lockheed Lightning aircraft, 128, 143-4

ARABIA PAST AND PRESENT

BOOKS FROM OLEANDER

ARABIAN GULF INTELLIGENCE
comp. R.H. Thomas
ISBN 0 900891 54 8

BANGKOK: Portrait of a City
Philip Ward
ISBN 0 902675 44 3

BEFRIENDING: A Sociological Case-History
M. Hagard & V. Blickem
ISBN 0 900891 27 0

A DOCTOR IN SAUDI ARABIA
G.E. Moloney
ISBN 0 906672 81 3

FINNISH CITIES (Helsinki, Turku, Tampere, and
Lapland)
Philip Ward
ISBN 0 906672 98 8

HA'IL: Oasis City of Saudi Arabia
Philip Ward
ISBN 0 900891 75 0

INDONESIAN TRADITIONAL POETRY
Philip Ward
ISBN 0 902675 49 4

JAPANESE CAPITALS (Nara, Kyoto, Tokyo)
Philip Ward
ISBN 0 906672 88 0

MINISTER IN OMAN
Neil McLeod Innes
ISBN 0 900891 89 0

POLISH CITIES (Cracow, Gdańsk & Malbork, Warsaw)
Philip Ward
ISBN 0 906672 73 2

RAJASTHAN, AGRA, DELHI: A Travel Guide
Philip Ward
ISBN 0 906672 44 9

ROSSYA: A Journey through Siberia
Michael Pennington
ISBN 0 906672 10 4

SUDAN TALES
Rosemary Kenrick
ISBN 0 906672 31 7

TRAVELS IN OMAN
Philip Ward
ISBN 0 906672 51 1